SNEAKERS

DRESS, BODY, CULTURE

Series Editor: **Joanne B. Eicher, *Regents' Professor, University of Minnesota***

Advisory Board:

Djurdja Bartlett, *London College of Fashion, University of the Arts*
Pamela Church-Gibson, *London College of Fashion, University of the Arts*
James Hall, *University of Illinois at Chicago*
Vicki Karaminas, *University of Technology, Sydney*
Gwen O'Neal, *University of North Carolina at Greensboro*
Ted Polhemus, *Curator, "Street Style" Exhibition, Victoria and Albert Museum*
Valerie Steele, *The Museum at the Fashion Institute of Technology*
Lou Taylor, *University of Brighton*
Karen Tranberg Hansen, *Northwestern University*
Ruth Barnes, *Ashmolean Museum, University of Oxford*

Books in this provocative series seek to articulate the connections between culture and dress which is defined here in its broadest possible sense as any modification or supplement to the body. Interdisciplinary in approach, the series highlights the dialogue between identity and dress, cosmetics, coiffure and body alternations as manifested in practices as varied as plastic surgery, tattooing, and ritual scarification. The series aims, in particular, to analyze the meaning of dress in relation to popular culture and gender issues and will include works grounded in anthropology, sociology, history, art history, literature, and folklore.

ISSN: 1360-466X

Previously published in the Series

Helen Bradley Foster, *"New Raiments of Self": African American Clothing in the Antebellum South*
Claudine Griggs, *S/he: Changing Sex and Changing Clothes*
Michaele Thurgood Haynes, *Dressing Up Debutantes: Pageantry and Glitz in Texas*
Anne Brydon and Sandra Niessen, *Consuming Fashion: Adorning the Transnational Body*
Dani Cavallaro and Alexandra Warwick, *Fashioning the Frame: Boundaries, Dress and the Body*

SNEAKERS

Fashion, Gender, and Subculture

YUNIYA KAWAMURA

Bloomsbury Academic
An imprint of Bloomsbury Publishing Plc

B L O O M S B U R Y
LONDON · OXFORD · NEW YORK · NEW DELHI · SYDNEY

Bloomsbury Academic

An imprint of Bloomsbury Publishing Plc

50 Bedford Square	1385 Broadway
London	New York
WC1B 3DP	NY
UK	10018 USA

www.bloomsbury.com

BLOOMSBURY and the Diana logo are trademarks of Bloomsbury Publishing Plc

First published 2016
Reprinted 2016, 2017

© Yuniya Kawamura, 2016

British Library Cataloguing-in-Publication Data
A catalogue record for this book is available from the British Library.

ISBN: HB: 978-0-8578-5722-4
PB: 978-0-8578-5733-0
ePDF: 978-1-4742-6292-7
ePub: 978-1-4742-6293-4

Library of Congress Cataloging-in-Publication Data
Kawamura, Yuniya, 1963-
Sneakers : fashion, gender, and subculture / Yuniya Kawamura.
pages cm. – (Dress, body, culture)
ISBN 978-0-85785-722-4 (hardback) – ISBN 978-0-85785-733-0 (paperback)
1. Sneakers. 2. Sneakers–Social aspects. I. Title.
GV749.S64R38 2016
685'.31–dc23
2015025895

Series: Dress, Body, Culture

Typeset by Integra Software Services Pvt. Ltd.
Printed and bound in Great Britain

To My Family

CONTENTS

LIST OF ILLUSTRATIONS

Disclaimer: This publication is not endorsed, approved, sponsored, or affiliated with any of the brand owners/sneaker manufacturers that feature herein. All brands, logos, trademarks, and series marks featured in this publication are used by way of nominative fair use only for the purposes of criticism, review, comparison, and/or as a point of reference in this academic publication.

Plates

All photographs by the author.

Graphs and Tables

ACKNOWLEDGMENTS

My appreciation goes to all the sneaker enthusiasts, fans, and collectors in New York who shared with me their stories, experiences, and passions for sneakers, and also to those who agreed their sneakers to be photographed by the author. This book would not have been possible without their contributions. I take my hat off to their unwavering passion for sneakers, and respect goes to all the sneaker enthusiasts around the world.

I am grateful to all my colleagues in the Social Sciences Department at the Fashion Institute of Technology (FIT), Lou Zaera, Ernie Poole, Margaret Miele, Joseph Maiorca, Yasemin Celik, Roberta Paley, Paul Clement, Praveen Chaudhry, Emre Ozsoz, Dan Benkendorf, Jung-Whan (Marc) de Jong, Gennady Lyakir, and Dan Levinson-Wilk for their collegial support. Students in my classes at FIT, "Clothing and Society," "Cultural Expressions of Non-Western Dress/ Fashion," and "Youth Subcultures, Identity and Fashion" provided a valuable sounding board for the development of my ideas, and they continue to inspire me as we share the same love for fashion.

I have given a number of presentations on my sneaker research at academic conferences in and outside the United States: "A Systemic Approach to Fashion and Dress with/without Visual Materials as Evidence" at *the Producing the History of Fashion in the West Conference* at the Museum of Decorative Arts in Paris, France; "Academic Research on Footwear" at *the Fashion: Exploring Critical Issues Global Conference*, at Mansfield College, Oxford University, UK; and "The Legitimation of Street Art/Artists through Sneaker Designs" at *the European Sociological Association (ESA) Conference*, the University of Turin, Italy. These trips were partially funded by FIT's Faculty Development Grants and Awards Program (FDGA) as well as the Liberal Arts Dean's Office. I owe special thanks to them.

I thank all the schools and symposium/conference organizers that invited me to give a presentation on this book prior to its completion, such as at *the Fashion Studies Today: History, Theory and Practice Conference* at New York University; the *Fashion and Creativity* Summer Program at the University of Bologna (Rimini branch), Italy; and *the Fashion Business Program Symposium* at Meiji University in Tokyo, Japan.

This is the fifth book that I am publishing from Berg/Bloomsbury, and it is always a pleasure working with their efficient and professional editorial team, especially Hannah Crump and Ariadne Godwin. I am immensely grateful for their patience.

I am indebted to all my former colleagues and friends at the Nihon Keizai Shimbun (Nikkei) who gave me the opportunity to write about fashion in their publications twenty years ago when I did not know anything about fashion writing, but that eventually led me to graduate school, major in sociology, and write a PhD dissertation on fashion and sociology. They have asked me to write a fashion column about sneakers in the evening edition of Nikkei.

My gratitude also goes to my research assistant in Tokyo, Hideki Shimizu, for collecting and putting together tabulated data. I also thank the gracious assistance provided by the library staff at Columbia University and FIT.

I also thank my friends, Lisa Okubo, who helped me with the administrative process of this project and gave me advice and suggestions on numerous occasions, and Laura Sidorowicz, who was constantly in touch with me to check my stress level when I was swamped with multiple projects and deadlines.

Finally, I dedicate this book to my family, Yoya, Yoko, and Maya Kawamura, who have always been supportive of my work. I could not have completed this book without their love and encouragement.

Yuniya Kawamura
New York

INTRODUCTION: PLACING SNEAKERS WITHIN SOCIOLOGY

Sneakers: Fashion, Gender, and Subculture is the first academic book dedicated solely to sneakers written by a sociologist. It is an in-depth theoretical and conceptual analysis of cultural, social, aesthetic, and economic interpretations of sneakers, and these external socio-structural factors inevitably influence personal and subjective meanings attached to the object and practices and experiences derived from it. I make an attempt to show that sneakers as a theme can or should be included in a sociological debate and discourse, and it can be investigated from multiple theoretical approaches and perspectives. Objects and artifacts, especially consumer products, that are useful in our everyday life and that originated in popular and mass culture are often devalued and neglected by scholars, but I argue that sneakers as a legitimate research focus deserves serious attention and worthwhile considerations by the research community. Sneakers, like other types of footwear, are more than an object that covers one's feet, and they can be identified as a subculture, a status symbol, a fashion item, and a modern and a postmodern social/cultural object that binds a community and people together among others.

Giorgio Riello in his thorough study of footwear of the eighteenth century, *A Foot in the Past* (2006), explains:

> Footwear is a garment characterized by a long history. In prehistoric times, it was a simple piece of wood or leather and was used to protect the foot. Today shoes are more than functional objects. They convey a wide range of meanings associated with fashion, style, personality, sexuality, gender, and class. (Riello 2006: 1)

Similarly, Valerie Steele, who writes extensively on high heels, also remarks: "[S]hoes convey a wealth of information about an individual's sexuality, social status, and aesthetic sensibility ... shoes unquestionably have tremendous social and psychological power" (Steele 2013: 7). I wish to investigate what these social and psychological powers are in regard to sneakers and shed light on this object that has been getting social recognition in the past few decades.

Furthermore, a group of sneaker enthusiasts have established a persistent male-dominant community that excludes and alienates girls and women. Gender is visible and present in various ways through objects, places, and words among others. Sneakers represent manhood and masculinity. Material culture of gender creates and recreates gendered beings, and a pair of sneakers that is used in sports is in turn associated with men, and in which women are in the subordinate and secondary position. Boys and young men are the biggest consumers of sneakers. While clothing is becoming unisex and androgynous, shoes remain to be gender-specific in terms of their designs, colors, and sizes. Few realize that there are far more varieties and choices for male sneakers than female sneakers.

However, there is still a shortage of academic research on men's dress. McNeil and Karaminas explain:

> Insufficient attention has been paid to men's dress within fashion history, as in the social imagination women have been more closely equated with the consumption of fashion in the West, certainly in twentieth-century life.... Despite the recent interest in the "metrosexual" and the "new man," the convention that men have a radically different attitude toward their clothes is still present in much contemporary culture. (McNeil and Karaminas 2009: 1)

Similarly, Christopher Breward in his article "Fashioning Masculinity: Men's Footwear and Modernity" (2011) discusses the common misconception that people have about men and their interests or disinterests in outward appearance:

> Contrary to popular knowledge—which erroneously suggests that masculinity and clothes shopping are irreconcilable states—the acquisition of a pair of good shoes has long been counted among one of the most important considerations undertaken by any well-respecting male follower of fashion. Indeed for most men, regardless of their position on the seriousness of dress, the fitting of the feet in appropriate attire constitutes a commercial transaction deserving of at least their limited attention, if only for those reasons of comfort and value that tend to impinge less directly on the consumption of their items of clothing. (Breward 2011: 206–207)

No one can agree with Breward's statement more than those who first decide what to wear on their feet before their clothes every morning. Sneaker enthusiasts are identified by their footwear, so the shoes they wear everyday are crucial in defining who they are. They are meticulous about which pair to wear on which occasion, how to wear it, and how to tie their shoelaces. It is not their occupation or social background that shapes their identity. It is the sneakers that convey information about them. As one of the sneaker enthusiasts said to me:

> When I'm wearing my fresh pair of sneakers, it puts me on a different level. I am who I am because of my sneakers. I am what I wear on my feet. It's a feeling I can't describe. I feel so good inside. It's the feeling only the sneakerheads can understand. If you are not one of us, you won't understand how we feel about sneakers.

Wearing the "right" pair of sneakers elevates them socially, psychologically, and emotionally, and it literally puts them on a social pedestal within their community. They are consciously aware who the insiders are and who are not. What matters to them most is their peers' opinions, and they constantly hunt and chase after the pair that earns them respect and reputation. A collector who has almost 800 pairs secretly admits:

> The more sneakers you have, the more respect you earn from your peers. A number of sneakers you have does matter because if you have as many pairs as I do, you need a place or a room to store them. Apartments are expensive, especially in New York. I have one room just for sneakers! We often buy two or three pairs of the same style. It means we have the money to buy so many. One to wear, one to keep for a special event, and for some people, one to sell on E-bay. It's not like I buy any sneakers just to increase my collection. The ones I have are all rare and exclusive. Personally, I never auction my sneakers. True sneakerheads should never sell their sneakers. If you really love sneakers, you would keep them to yourself. For me, it's not business. For some people, it is.

Sneakers are a subtle and a latent expression of conspicuous consumption. The general public would not recognize their value, and only the insiders are able to share the meaning, and that is the very reason that the community can be called a "subculture."

I see similarities between sneaker enthusiasts and the British dandies in the Regency period whose aim is to be recognized only by his peers. As Vainshtein explains (2009: 97): "[T]his recognition has to rely on discreet signs. That is why the details become the leading semiotic code in men's costume of the Regency period—hence the necessity of magnifying visual devices for scrutinizing the subtle details and judging the appropriateness of them."

This book gives a clear picture and an understanding of how sneaker enthusiasts began to construct an informal network group in a virtual as well as a physical space, and how their passions for sneakers have been produced, reproduced, spread, expanded, and maintained over the years through competition. It also looks at sneaker collection, hunting, and trading as a social phenomenon and treats sneaker enthusiasts and their communities as a subcultural group that transformed mere athletic footwear into fashion, and this idea of "fashion" is the key concept in the male-dominant sneaker subculture.

A few scholars have argued that the race factor is often neglected in subcultural studies. Dylan Clark, in his article "The Death and Life of Punk, the Last Subculture" (2003), writes:

> From the flappers of the 1920s to the Chicano cholos of the 1970s, "subculture" is above all a container that attempts to hold various groups of young people whose affect, clothing, music and norms, deviate from a mythological centre. That these subcultures are often "White" in their ethnic composition is regularly unmarked in academic discussions, despite its enormous import. (Clark 2003: 223, footnote 2)

Mariana Böse also questions in her article "Where is the 'Black' in the Post-Subcultural Theory?" (2003: 167). Her analysis of a subculture is focused on race and class, and she interviews cultural practitioners who are mostly of Afro-Caribbean descent, in which many of them talk about the appropriation of Black coolness that is exploited by White subcultures.

On the other hand, David Muggleton (1997: 199) offers a postmodern interpretation of style as "no longer articulated around the modernist structuring relations of class, gender, ethnicity or even the age span of 'youth,'" and I concur with his viewpoint that stylistic heterogeneity has been pushed to its utmost limits as the outward appearance of rebellion becomes merely another mode of fashion (Muggleton 1997: 195). He implies that there is no sense of subcultural authenticity. Therefore, although race as a variable has not completely disappeared among the sneaker enthusiasts, I do not focus on the race factor of the sneaker subculture in this book which has been diversified and is now spreading to all cultures, classes, ages, races, and ethnic groups.

Although the sneaker community contains many of the determinants of a subculture, no scholar has ever conducted sociological or anthropological research specifically about them, while there are numerous journalistic writings, websites, and blogs on the topic since footwear, including sneakers, is a huge industry.

My theoretical applications and explorations are based on my empirical work, and I make a contribution to various fields of discipline in academia, such as sociology, anthropology, cultural studies, subcultural studies, youth studies, media studies, gender studies, and fashion and dress studies. As an academic, it is my responsibility as a sociologist to shed light on topics and themes that are often forgotten, dismissed, and marginalized as unimportant. It is a way to raise awareness on both parties, the general public and the academics, and to bridge a gap between the two. Tangible objects all contain social meanings so long as they are situated and placed in our culture and society.

This book is intended for undergraduate/graduate students and scholars primarily in the above-mentioned social sciences discipline, who most probably do not know much about sneakers. In addition, those who study fashion design and fashion business, such as merchandizing and marketing, could also benefit from this book as it describes the social and institutional processes which sneakers go through to become a "fashion" item. The transition and the conversion of meanings attached to the sneakers from an athletic shoe to a shoe with adornment purposes and a status symbol are explained in detail. The growing popularity of sneakers led to the formation of a legitimate fashion genre called "streetwear," which Steven Vogel explains as follows:

> Streetwear represents a lifestyle that many agree was born in the early 1980s in New York. Due to the constant alienation and frustration felt mainly by inner city kids, not just in New York but worldwide, a community was formed that was influenced by skateboarding, punk, hardcore, reggae, hiphop, an emerging club culture, graffiti, travel and the art scene in downtown city centre areas. (Vogel 2006: 7)

It has a foundation in grassroots communities of like-minded people, and the styles are simple, comfortable, functional, practical, and much imitated a style of dress, and the streetwear stereotypes are expensive/rare sneakers, baggy denims, hoodies, and loose, emblazoned T-shirts (Sims 2010), all of which are initially based on hip-hop aesthetics.

Moreover, my research also clarifies the conceptual difference between a material object of dress, such as footwear, and an immaterial object, such as fashion, which is difficult to define and grasp. All the photographs of sneakers included in this book are taken by the author unless otherwise mentioned, and the purpose of these images is to show the readers the countless varieties and the incredible creativity of sneaker designs.

Even if a reader of this book never wears sneakers or has no interests in them, he or she will learn much from this seemingly mundane object because they are filled with multiple as well as complex layers and levels of ideas, attitudes, and beliefs. Sneakers are deep. They are much more than mere footwear. One of the young collectors said:

> Sneakers literally changed my life. Every night before I go to bed, I decide which pair I'm going to wear the next day so that I don't have to waste time in the morning trying to decide which one to wear. I always check the next day weather first. If it's going to rain the next day, I don't want to wear anything white or light colors because the last thing sneakerheads want to do is to damage the kicks in the rain. Rain is a nightmare for us! If you want to sell your kicks in the future, you don't want to wear it in the rain. We wanna keep them as fresh as possible.

I saw this firsthand when I attended the SneakerCon in December, 2014, in New York when it was pouring rain all day, and I saw a couple of sneaker enthusiasts putting plastic shopping bags over their sneakers to make sure they do not get wet. One of the boys standing in line to get inside the convention center said:

> This is the worst day for sneakerheads. You want to wear your best kicks to impress your friends at an event like this, but you don't want to ruin your sneakers in this torrential rain.

Wearing blue denim may also stain the sneakers. Another sneaker collector explains ways to protect them:

> You put a piece of gum tape at the hem of your jeans because the blue denim sometimes stains your sneakers. You don't want that especially on your favorite white kicks so if the bottom edge of your jeans touches your sneakers, you cover it with some tape.

For many sneaker enthusiasts, their life revolves around sneakers. They live for sneakers. They work for sneakers and spend most of their income on sneakers. They spend every hour and every minute of the day checking sneaker-related information on their smartphones. A salesperson at a sneaker store said:

> People always say you should do what you love in life and follow your true passion, don't they? Sneakers have been my passion since grammar school. Sneakers are my passion. There's no doubt about it so I've planned my career path around sneakers. I first worked in the stockroom filled with sneaker merchandise, and I could learn everything about new sneakers that were coming into the store. Then I was promoted to a salesperson on the floor. And I obviously spent all my paychecks on sneakers. They are my babies.

I do not pretend to be a sneaker expert who knows the name, the history, the background, and the technical production process of each and every sneaker that has ever been released. I will leave that up to those who are known as the sneaker connoisseurs and/or designers, such as Bobbito Garcia, Ronnie Fieg, Jeff Staple, Jeff Harris, Eugene Kan, Pete Forester, and Yuming Wu among others.[1] My personal interactions and encounters with them and many other sneaker fans and collectors have further raised my sociological curiosity about sneakers. The more I listened to their personal stories, passions, and experiences, the more interested I became in the sneaker world and the industries that helped grow and expand this fascinating subculture. I assure my readers that after reading this book, their views on sneakers will change forever as much as they did for me during the process of my own research.[2]

Sneakers and youth subcultures within sociology

C. Wright Mills' *Sociological Imagination* (1959) enables us to look at the larger sociohistorical scene in regard to individual personal lives, and it allows us to grasp history and biography and the relations between the two within society which can be analyzed from macro and micro perspectives. As Mills explains, no social study that does not come back to the problems of biography, of history, and of their intersections within a society has intellectual significance, and neither the life of an individual nor the history of a society can be understood without understanding both. Scholars have not yet explained a sneaker phenomenon from an intellectual viewpoint as Mills would suggest. We can make a transformative shift from a subjective and personal perspective of sneaker enthusiasts to a larger sneaker community within a wider society, which is impersonal and institutional. There is a structure of the sneaker network that is being solidified over the years with the help of the industry and technology as well as individuals who interact with one another through the role they play as a sneaker enthusiast.

Therefore, I locate sneakers within a sociological framework to make an analysis of a group of fans and collectors that make up a sneaker subculture that appears to be separate from the mainstream dominant society. I treat sneakers not only as a material object but also as an immaterial object, the two of which are inextricably interrelated to create the mental concept of an object.

Furthermore, my work also fills a void in footwear studies. Shoes have been a crucial part of the wardrobe throughout history. Starting with the practical need to protect from outside elements, shoes began to carry other purposes. There is a wide range of footwear types and designs found throughout the world in many different cultures. However, there are less interests in contemporary male footwear, and Breward's "Fashioning Masculinity: Men's Footwear and Modernity" (2011: 206–223) is one of the few studies on this topic. Contemporary male footwear does not appear to have much aesthetic functions or psychosexual meanings like female shoes, and researchers as well as the general public pay less attention to them. With sneakers, there is even less serious focus as people tend to look at them only from a utilitarian viewpoint, and they are worn mainly for sports and appear to have no other social functions.

My attempt is not to simply explain a phenomenon of sneakers but to look at it as a social object that is imbued with a great deal of interpretations. A practical cultural object, such as sneakers, represents different facets of current society with implications and symbolism. I investigate the transformation of values that is socially constructed, the macro and micro interconnection between sneaker fans and major sneaker manufacturers, and how an object is turned into a fashion object.

My research on sneakers is also an extension of my previous work on the sociological investigation of Japanese youth subcultures and their stylistic expressions (Kawamura 2012). For scholars who are fascinated by distinct outward appearance, youth subcultures are of our particular interests because their dress and actions are unique and unconventional. I share my thoughts with Angela McRobbie, who explains her interest in subcultures as follows:

> There are two reasons why I have been interested in subcultures: first, because they have always appeared to me … as popular aesthetic movements, or "constellations" … and second, because in a small way they have seemed to possess the capacity to change the direction of young people's lives, or at least to sharpen their focus by confirming some felt, but as yet unexpressed intent or desire. Subcultures are aesthetic movements whose raw materials are by definition, "popular" in that they are drawn from the world of the popular mass media. It is not necessary to have an education in the *avant-garde* or to know the history of surrealism to enjoy the Sex Pistols or to recognize the influence of Vivienne Westwood's fashion. This kind of knowledge (of pop music or fashion images) is relatively easy to come by and very different from the knowledge of the high arts or the literary canon found in the academy. (McRobbie 1991: xv)

We learn much from youth subcultures about their worldviews and ideologies through their actions and dress which are manifested verbally and nonverbally. Their social messages are often transmitted through their clothes since fashion is a nonlinguistic mode of communication. We can read a great deal of latent messages in the way they dress, and sometimes the wearers themselves are not even aware of the impact of these hidden ideas that they are subconsciously spreading to the world.

Several years ago, when I was lecturing on subcultural theories in my class, one of my students asked: "Is a group of sneakers considered a subculture also?" That was the first time I had ever heard about a sneaker subculture, and she recommended me a documentary DVD called "Just for Kicks" (2005) directed by Thibaut de Longeville and Lisa Leone which is a "must-watch" among the sneaker enthusiasts. It captures well the sneaker scenes in New York City and shows how a sneaker subculture initially emerged as an underground community and as part of hip-hop culture. It immediately gripped my interests in this topic. Until then, like many others, I had looked at sneakers only as athletic shoes worn for sports or as part of casualwear. When I found out about the existence of a community of sneaker enthusiasts, I was so mesmerized by them that I wanted to know more. The sneaker community has expanded tremendously after this documentary, and it has gained the attention of high fashion houses, such as Chanel, Givenchy, and Louis Vuitton, which are now manufacturing expensive sneakers.

Our goal as sociologists is to discover the pattern across subcultures and answer theoretical questions about subcultures in general, and we make an attempt to place a subculture group in a larger theoretical framework and examine its exclusive placement within a society. Subcultures are often treated as nonmainstream or antiestablishment with values and norms that represent the groups and are believed to deviate from the conventional ones. I explore the commonalities and uniqueness of the sneaker subculture in comparison to other subcultures that had already been sociologically analyzed.

Subcultural ethnography as an outsider/ insider researcher

In youth and subcultural research, there are always questions about the position of a researcher in relation to his/her research subjects. As Rhoda MacRae in her "'Insider' and 'Outsider' Issues in Youth Research" points out:

> With the multiplicities of identity being widely recognized within sociology, youth researchers, amongst others, have also begun to reconsider insider-outsider distinctions....Ethnographic research provides the context for many of the discussions about insider and outsider positions in social research. The position of research in relation to the group under study has been a classical dilemma in qualitative, and particularly, ethnographic research into cultural formations. The social and cultural proximity or distance of the researcher from the researched have been of interest ever since Weber developed the notion of *verstehen*, which translates from German as understanding. (MacRae 2007: 51–52)

There are pros and cons to conducting research as an insider or an outsider. Both have advantages and disadvantages. MacRae (2007: 53–56) suggests that there are three approaches: outsider-in, outsider-out, and insider-in. The outsider-in method allows the researcher to learn about the life of others through observation and experience from the position of a stranger while the outsider-out approach pays less empirical attention on the research subject by employing external textual analysis and having no and little direct interaction with the research subject (MacRae 2007: 53–54). The insider-in perspective is taken by a researcher who is a member of the group that he or she is studying. A number of scholars who study various types and forms of youth subcultures were the insider members at one point in their life (Bennett and Hodkinson 2012; Haenfler 2006, 2009, 2014; Hodkinson 2002; Muggleton 2000). For instance, Hodkinson (2002), who himself is part of the Goth subculture, conducted research on the Goth scene in Britain for a number of years, and as an insider member, he knows how he should dress, which music to listen to, and which magazines and novels to read, to be part of the subculture. But he explains his complex position within the subculture as an insider with subjective viewpoints and a researcher that requires objectivity:

> Indeed, in some respects my insider status was actually enhanced, as the project was built around an intensified attendance of clubs, gigs and festivals across Britain…. Participation on internet discussion groups and other goth internet facilities widened the scope of my research within Britain, and was the main source of my more limited information and contacts outside the country. Whether off- or on-line, the authenticity of my participation greatly enhanced the process of acquiring contacts, interviewees and information. As well as having a suitable appearance, the manner in which I behaved in clubs—dancing, requesting songs from DJs and socializing—made meeting people, arranging interviews, taking photographs and gaining advice far easier than they might otherwise have been. (Hodkinson 2002: 5)

After all, despite the emphasis on objectivity in social sciences, the very first step of selecting a topic, spending years researching the topic, and writing about it demands a great deal of time, money, and passion. As a result, it is no surprise that some decide to pick a subject that they are most familiar with or are very much involved in. Muggleton applies Weberian interpretation of meaning to his study of a subcultural phenomena and emphasizes the significance of subjectivity and also the social factors that influence the meanings that each individual creates. He writes:

> [A] Weberian study of subculture must be based upon an interpretation of the subjectively held meanings, values and beliefs of the subculturalists themselves. This is the premise upon which Weber's *verstehen* methodology is founded, the literal translation of the term *verstehen* being "human understanding"…. We must therefore take seriously the subjective meanings of subculturalists, for these provide the motivation for their conduct. This makes the subjective dimension a central component in any explanation of social phenomena. (Muggleton 2000: 10)

In my research on sneakers, I have played a role between the outsider-out and the outsider-in. I admit that conducting this research was in a way challenging since I am a female and the majority of the sneaker enthusiasts are boys and young men. But as professional researchers in the research community know, sometimes it is an advantage to be an outsider since I am a bystander or a stranger to the group from their perspective, and that is why I am able to find out what is distinct about sneaker enthusiasts and what is different from the mainstream society. As an outsider, one can also experience firsthand how the insiders treat the outsiders. I do not personally share their passion and values, nor do I follow their code, and there was always an assumption on their part that I do not share their "subcultural knowledge" (Thornton 1995). My views are completely objective when I look at sneakers or speak to the members of the subculture. I do not make any personal judgments on different types of sneakers that they have on their feet, although I have come to know their social differences. But as an attempt to fit in, I made my sneakers a little creative by stitching the face of a handmade teddy bear on my sneakers which some sneaker fans thought was the famous adidas pair designed by Jeremy Scott.

The empirical part of my research was conducted through fieldwork. I have talked to sneaker designers, collectors, writers, and retailers that sell expensive and cheap sneakers. I have attended sneaker events, such as conventions, visited stores in New York, London, and Tokyo (but this book is mostly about New York). I have closely followed and read tweets, Instagrams, and blogs that all were related to sneakers. I have visited popular sneaker webzines and auction sites that release sneaker-related information and buy and sell sneakers.

A background of the sneaker industry

We all have at least one pair of sneakers in our shoe closet and do not think much of it since sneakers never used to hold a high social status in the footwear hierarchy. It is comfortable and functional. Unlike the high-heeled shoes that symbolized power and superior social status (see Chapter 1), sneakers are flat and the sole is mostly made out of rubber which is easy to manage and inexpensive to manufacture. Nor do they have any erotic appeal to attract the public. Sneakers were never thought of as a fetish object. We have treated sneakers simply as an object we put on our feet. However, no matter how much we are fascinated by female high-heel shoes, the bond of the collectors is not strong enough to create a subculture of their own; they do not mobilize to form a tight-knit group and trade their high-heels, or camp outside a shoe store when limited editions come out. We do not know of any footwear items that bind people together as much as the sneaker enthusiasts do. It is that one item of dress that unites the whole community not only in New York but also globally. The world of sneakers is increasingly becoming institutionalized with regular sneaker releases, blogs, tweets, Instagram updates events, stores, publications, and websites, all of which provide a space for the members to congregate and mobilize.

Vanderbilt writes (1998: 2): "Call it a sneaker, call it an athletic shoe. That lightweight bundle of polymer and plastic, leather and lace is more than just footwear." Sneakers were worn by celebrities in special events and occasions: Mick Jagger was married in sneakers; Woody Allen wore sneakers when he escorted First Lady Betty Ford to the ballet; Jackie Onasis and Mickey Rooney wore European-made sneakers (Zimmerman 1978: 7). More recently, an article in the *New York Times* (Blumenthal 2015: E3) says: "As Fashion Week comes to town on Thursday, the streets will fill with look-at-me style statements. But fewer of those, we suspect, will be ratcheted to the heavens on sky-high heels. It's all about sneakers now." Fashion professionals who attend the Fashion Week were always seen in decorative high-heels, but that trend has been changing. Sneakers that used to play a minor role in the world of fashion are now playing a main character on stage.

Business and trade newspapers and magazines cover the sneaker industry on a regular basis because it is an important part of the fashion industry. According to the National Shoe Retailers Association, the footwear industry's total revenue in 2014 was US$48 billion, while the American consumer spending on footwear was US$20 billion.[3] Of all the shoe categories, men's athletic shoes have the biggest market share of 20 percent followed by women's casual shoes of 17 percent and women's dress shoes of 13 percent (see Graph 1).

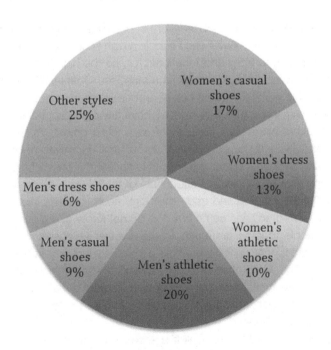

Graph 1 Shoe Category Market Share (2014).

As people's lifestyles and dresses became increasingly casual, there were more occasions and opportunities for people to wear sneakers besides playing sports. Major sneaker manufacturers include Nike, adidas (always with a lower case "a"), Puma, New Balance, Converse (now owned by Nike), Reebok, Fila, Vans, and Keds. Each company has its unique history and background, and they all have trademark sneakers that have left an indelible mark in the sneaker history.

It was Keds and Converse that laid the first foundation of the sneaker manufacturing producing specialized footwear for athletes in the early twentieth century. Converse remained a leader in the industry with its All Star sneakers until the mid-1950s. Although it later lost its momentum and was acquired by Nike in 2003, it is still considered one of the most iconic items that changed the history of style (Rocca 2013: 94–99) along with Levi's jeans, Tiffany pearls, Burberry raincoats, and LaCoste shirts. New Balance started as a company that sold arch support for shoes and started making sneakers only in the 1960s; the brand has unique size variations for the width of a foot. Reebok, initially called Boulton, has an old history since 1890 in the United Kingdom with making spike running shoes that were new at the time. Vans is a company that was established in 1966 by Paul Van Doren and remains to be very popular among skateboarders because of thick soles which make the shoes durable. Asics, a Japanese company formerly known as Onitsuka, had an earlier connection with Nike which dates back to 1963 when Phil Knight visited Japan and decided to import and sell their sneakers in the United States (see Table 1).[4]

Table 1 *Major Sneaker Companies by Country and Year Established*

Year established	Country	Company name
1890	UK	Boulton (later changed to Reebok)
1906	USA	New Balance (started making sneakers in the 1960s)
1908	USA	Converse (acquired by Nike in 2003)
1917	USA	Keds
1924	Germany	Gebrüder-Dassler Schuhfabrik (split into Puma and adidas)
1946	Germany	adidas
1948	Germany	Puma
1949	Japan	Asics (formerly called Onitsuka)
1958	UK	Reebok (formerly called Boulton; acquired by adidas in 2005)

Year established	Country	Company name
1963	USA	Blue Ribbon Sports (later changed to Nike)
1966	USA	Vans
1972	USA	Nike

Source: Various publications and websites.

The current athletic footwear industry is dominated by three companies, Nike, adidas, and Puma, of which Nike has been a top runner. According to statista. com, in 2014, the total revenue was US$16.2 billion for Nike, followed by US$8.1 billion for adidas, and US$1.56 billion for Puma. Nike's popularity was apparent from my field observation in New York as well. The majority of the photos I have taken for the book were randomly shot on the streets, at the stores, and the sneaker conventions, and they were mostly Nike sneakers, such as Air Jordan or Lebron James.

Of Nike's total footwear revenue in 2014, the majority comes from North America with US$ 7.5 billion, US$ 3.3 billion come from Western Europe, and US$ 2.6 billion from emerging markets, such as Mexico and Brazil. Nike was initially called Blue Ribbon Sport established by Phil Knight, a member of the University of Oregon track team, and Bill Bowerman, his track coach. After importing and distributing running sneakers from Japan, they set out to create their own sneakers in 1972 and changed the company name to Nike. By the end of the 1970s, they were making sneakers for other sports in addition to track and field and aggressively expanding their business to other sports. It is not only one of the youngest sneaker companies in the industry but also the largest and is the leader since it became a publicly traded company in 1980.

Nike is followed by adidas whose footwear division generates the revenue with US$ 8.1 billion selling 258 million pairs of shoes. Their largest regional market was the emerging Eastern European markets which accounted for 38 percent of net sales. In comparison to Nike and adidas, Puma's sales growth has been stable and steady since 2006. Footwear is their most profitable segment with US$ 1.2 billion revenues in 2014 followed by apparels (http://www.statista.com/statistics/278834/revenue-nike-adidas-puma-footwear-segmen).

The story of Puma and adidas very much reflects a competitive nature of the industry. It was in 1920 that two German brothers, Adolph and Rudolf Dassler, started their company called Gebrüder-Dassler Schuhfabrik and made their first shoe. They earned their reputation after Jesse Owens wore Dassler shoes and won the Olympics in 1936. However, sibling rivalry split the company into two separate companies. In 1946, Adolph set up his own company called adidas. Its two main logos are three parallel stripes and a three leaves trefoil mark. Adidas Superstar is a basketball shoe introduced in 1969, nicknamed as "shell toe," which is an adidas classic and is still the best-selling shoe.

In 1948, Ruldolf set up a company of his own across town from his brother's company and named it Puma. In the 1950s and 1960s, the company continued to endorse athletes in the Olympics and raised their reputation. In 1952, Josef Barthel of Luxembourg won the Olympic Gold medal in the 1,500 meters in Helsinki wearing a pair of Puma shoes. When an American track star, Tommie Smith, won the Gold Medal in the 200 meters and was on the stand, he raised his fist as a sign of racial inequality while leaving his Puma on the stand. Although he and his teammate were expelled because of this action, it brought a lot of media attention to the Puma suedes, which is a Puma classic and is one of their long-lasting popular sneakers. It was in 1968 that the company introduced the cat logo which became a trademark of Puma.

Sneaker companies contribute to sustaining the subculture of sneakers by constantly launching new editions. They realize that there is a market for youths who are hungry for cool and fashionable sneakers. In the subsequent chapters, I investigate the changing nature of the sneaker community from the 1970s to present with a major turning point in the mid-1980s with the launch of the Nike Air Jordan sneaker series. Once a subculture is commercialized, it begins to emerge from underground and surfaces on the upperground (see Chapter 2), and for some hardcore collectors, that is a disappointing outcome of the wide diffusion which is unstoppable with today's technology. Furthermore, the gender and fashion components of the subculture are explored as sneaker fans are almost always men, and they compete in acquiring the latest, limited edition sneakers. Sneaker enthusiasts are the most fashionable groups of people. They always feel the need and the urge to be "in fashion."

Literature on sneakers

There are a number of books that are heavily illustrated and written by and for sneaker enthusiasts. Despite the growing sneaker popularity in the 1980s, we did not see the first publication on sneakers until the late 1990s. The first comprehensive nonacademic book about the contemporary sneaker phenomenon is probably Tom Vanderbilt's *The Sneaker Book: Anatomy of an Industry and an Icon* (1998), which talks about the history of sneakers, the background of major sneaker manufacturers, marketing strategies to sell sneakers, and the social environments that surround the sneaker development. Then, in 2003, *Where'd You Get Those? New York City's Sneaker Culture: 1960–1987* (2003) was written by Bobbito Garcia, who is known as the father of the sneaker subculture. Garcia traces the history of sneakers since the 1960s when sneaker collection was still an underground practice. The book comprises of stories and anecdotes told by a first person, Garcia himself, about his personal experiences and attachment to the sneakers.

Since Garcia's publication, we see more publications dedicated exclusively to sneakers because that is what the fans and collectors go after. Unorthodox Style published *Sneakers: The Complete Collector's Guide* (2005) and *Sneakers: The Complete Limited Editions Guide* (2014). Neal Heard, a well-known sneaker connoisseur, has published a numbers of books: *The Trainers* (2003); *Sneakers* (2005), *Sneakers (Special Limited Edition): Over 300 Classics from Rare Vintage to the Latest Designs* (2009), and *The Sneaker Hall of Fame: All-Time Favorite Footwear Brands* (2012). All of his books provide detailed profiles and backgrounds of popular sneakers brands, including Nike, Converse, Fila, New Balance, and Puma, among many others.

Ben Osborne, editor of a popular basketball magazine, has published *SLAM Kicks: Baseball Sneakers that Changed the Game* (Osborne 2014). *Art & Sole: Contemporary Sneaker Art & Design* (2012) was published by Intercity, a graphic design studio, and it focuses exclusively on contemporary, cutting-edge sneaker design, and explores the creative side of sneaker culture showing the most original items and collaborations. These publications are written by sneaker experts and connoisseurs for sneaker fans and collectors and are not academic in nature, which is an indication that sneakers as a topic in academic research is overlooked or neglected in spite of their complex and powerful sociocultural meanings.

Shoes: A History from Sandals to Sneakers (2011), edited by Riello and McNeil, is the first book that compiles articles specifically written about footwear by academics. The book traces the cultural history of footwear both in the West and the East, and it attempts to contextualize shoes within a long history stretching over several centuries. Such a book motivates us fashion scholars to further investigate and make a contribution to this new research territory. One of the articles "Limousine for the Feet: The Rhetoric of Sneakers" by Allison Gill (2011: 372–385) discusses the sneaker industry in which she talks about the advancement of technology used in sneakers in creating an elite shoe, but there is no mentioning of gender, subculture, or fashion. Gill focuses on the production and the producers' side of sneakers, while I mainly examine the consumption aspect of sneakers. My intention is to explain and elaborate on how sneakers can be conceptualized from sociological perspectives.

Outline of the book

This book consists of six chapters. Chapter 1 gives an introduction to footwear studies as that will provide us with the overall understanding of how footwear has been analyzed from historical, sociological, political, and religious perspectives among others. It traces the past and the recent academic research on footwear. While fashion and dress studies often include only clothes, there are some outstanding scholarly research on footwear, such as Italian *chopines* and Japanese *geta* and *zori*. From these studies, we see that footwear was never just for functional purposes.

Chapters 2–4 examine theoretical discussions on sneakers in addition to my empirical work and analyze sneakers primarily from three perspectives— subculture, gender, and fashion, by applying various social theories to explore and examine the popularity and the phenomenon of sneakers. Some of the research questions that I raise prior to my research are: Why can we call a sneaker community a subculture? Why do they collect sneakers? What is distinct about their subculture compared to others? How does the emergence of a sneaker subculture mean to a larger society? How do their values and norms differ from others? Why is it male-dominant? How is their hegemonic masculinity maintained and reproduced? How do the industries get involved in the sustenance of the subculture, and what do they benefit from each other?

In Chapter 2, subcultural and post-subcultural theories are addressed and applied to a group of sneaker enthusiasts, and it explains why and how this group of boys and young men first formed a subculture in New York City and its social and economic background that effectively led to its formation. Chapter 3 looks at footwear as a gendered object which has historically drawn a clear line between male and female shoes, and even today, they rarely overlap. Footwear is still an item of dress that is still very much separated by gender, and a significant number of research focuses on female footwear and foot as a sexual, fetish object. In addition, the chapter discusses the male dominance in the sneaker subculture, and how they compete and at the same time are bonded through face-to-face and virtual communication. Chapter 4 focuses on the fashion component of sneakers that are commodified by various institutions and explains how a mundane consumer product, such as sneakers, is transformed into fashion. In Chapter 5, Emile Durkheim's various theoretical frameworks are applied in analyzing the sneaker subculture. Lastly, the conclusion chapter examines the future possibilities and suggestions for further academic research on sneakers, footwear, and beyond, such as bare feet and ankles.

There are different terminologies for sneakers found in various publications, articles, and quotes, such as trainers, running shoes, tennis shoes, plimsolls, gym shoes, track shoes, kicks, runners, and les baskets, but in my own text, I will use only the term "sneakers" unless the word is taken from a quote.

1

ACADEMIC RESEARCH ON FOOTWEAR

Before I delve into my research on sneakers, I will review some of the significant studies on historical as well as contemporary footwear to see how they may conceptually fit into my analysis of sneakers. Footwear is a field within fashion and dress studies. A scholarly research on sneakers is another contribution to the recent scholarship in footwear studies. We can learn from them how footwear as a research topic was studied in the past and present; which type of footwear scholars have selected and focused on; what potential research opportunities exist for footwear studies in the future; how the study of footwear differs from other studies on fashion or clothing items, if there are any; and what is missing in the current studies on footwear.

Riello explains that, until recently, footwear has been considered as a marginal accessory, and even in museums, shoes were rarely considered as an integral part of dress for most of the twentieth century (Riello 2006: 1). Compared to dress, footwear has played a peripheral role in fashion and dress studies, and my attempt is to shed light on this particular type of footwear, sneakers, which is now playing a main role on the fashion stage among the male youths not only in New York but also around the world.

The intricate relationship between the role a person plays and his or her dress is evident today primarily in shoes. People change their footwear according to the role. Specific shoe styles have been designed for different everyday activities, such as traveling, going to school or work, playing sports, going to social or religious functions, and so on. Similarly, these styles vary according to one's sex, age, status, values, season, and geographic location.

Be it clothing or footwear, we put them both on our body, and it is a way to dress, adorn, and decorate our body. We can dissect footwear in the same way that we dissect clothing or dress. Ingrid Brenninkmeyer discusses three functions of dress in her *Sociology of Fashion* (1963): protection, modesty, and decoration. Protection is the most obvious, practical, and utilitarian function of clothing, dress, or footwear. They cover your physical bodies for protection from your environment, the heat, or cold. Modesty is also another function of dress and clothing. In the West, the idea of modesty or immodesty is very much tied to the idea of nakedness. If a body is unclothed or uncovered, it is immodest, while if it is clothed, it is considered to be modest. The definition of modesty varies from culture to culture. Wherever nakedness is not an embarrassment, some other behavior or status is considered shameful.

Among all the three theories of dress, the concept of decoration is the most widely spread and popular. And it is a social concept since people adorn themselves expecting that they will be seen by society. It is about self-display. We do not decorate or embellish our bodies when we are alone by ourselves. We dress up, put makeup on, wear contact lenses, wear perfume, brush our hair, and wear good looking shoes when we go outside knowing we will be passing by people who are going to watch us. Brenninkmeyer was primarily talking about dress, that is, clothing on our bodies, but they also apply to footwear. As Walford writes (2007: 9): "Footwear is primarily an invention of necessity to protect us from the elements. However, over the centuries, and in almost every culture, footwear has taken vastly different forms, providing that there is far more at play than mere protection. Footwear in the Western world is the foddler of fashion." He emphasizes the adornment function of footwear, which we call "fashion" which compliments human bodies and feet to add extra values. We will see in various academic studies all types of shoes that possess more than practical functions.

This chapter examines academic research on footwear to understand the social and cultural meanings and categories attached to different types of footwear. It traces the history of footwear to understand why and when human beings started to wear something on their feet, and it explores what footwear symbolizes in various cultural contexts at various time periods in history. By reviewing the literature on footwear studies, we can see whether some of the conceptual analysis of footwear can be applied later to sneaker studies or not. It will help us gain further insight into sneakers and to see where it can be placed in.

The sociocultural significance of footwear

Human beings have been covering their feet and wearing some form of footwear for centuries. While there are countless accounts on who created the first shoes or why/where they were first made, the primary common reason for wearing shoes was to protect feet from an unpleasant or dangerous natural environment. For instance, an American sailor's shoe in the nineteenth century was made out of hemp cord because it provided traction even when it was wet, and double rubber-walled insulated boots were made for the US military personnel to protect feet from extreme cold (McIver 1994). Shoes were invented out of necessity just like clothes. In addition, shoes communicate who we are, what we do for living, and how we think. At a time when slaves and lower classes were barefoot, shoes were worn by those in power and authority. As McNeil and Riello explain in their article "A Long Walk: Shoes, People and Place" (2011b: 12): "The very presence or absence of shoes is one of the most recorded facts in history .... Until recent times, a lack of shoes could be a fact of life even in the relatively prosperous Western world. And to the barefoot meant that all avenues of life were closed."

Similarly, in a non-western culture, Jain-Neubauer points out that it was a common practice in most of rural India, until half a century ago, to walk barefoot, and therefore, it would not be an exaggeration to generally describe India as a "barefoot country," but the Indian aristocracy have developed a taste for footwear in the early centuries of the Christian era (2000: 13).

As Edna Nahshon, in her article "Jews and Shoes," writes (2008: 15): "Shoes function as metonyms for personhood and as markers of identity both by choice and coercion. They are a rich source of information for a person's age and gender, occupation, economic and social status, and religious and ideological position, as well as a host of personal characteristics." They serve as a nonverbal mode of communication conveying social information about the wearer. Similarly, Sue Blundell in "Beneath Their Shining Feet: Shoes and Sandals in Classical Greece" traces back the history of shoes in Classical Greece and explains that while many paintings and sculptures depict men and women without shoes, footwear was the norm even in Ancient Greece (2011). During the Roman era, shoes were considered as much more than functional footwear: poets commemorated them in verses and lovers cherished their beloveds' shoes as dearly as their locks of hair (McIver 1994: 6). One of the earliest examples of footwear worn on the Indian subcontinent is a sandal made out of wood which was found around circa 200 BC (Jain-Neubauer 2000: 9). Footwear has a long history and is definitely not a modern invention.

Different academic studies on historical and contemporary footwear can be placed within fashion and dress studies and explore their sociocultural significance as well as religious implications to understand how footwear has been analyzed by scholars in history, cultural anthropology, and sociology. The study of footwear in academia is overlooked as it appears to play a secondary role in fashion and dress. I examine some of the sociological components attached to different types of footwear to examine whether they can be applied to a study on sneakers.

Footwear in fashion and dress studies

We often take it for granted that fashion and dress are more about clothes and less about accessories that supplement the clothes. And other items we put on are less significant because they have less social importance than clothes. Dress is not simply clothing or garments, but it encompasses everything that we humans put on our body. Joanne Eicher et al. (2008) define dress as something that involves all our five tactile senses, such as touching, seeing, hearing, smelling, and tasting. Dressing oneself is not merely about putting on clothes:

> We view dress as a product and as a process that distinguishes human beings from other animals. As a product, many items are involved in dress that are a result of human creativity and technology. As a process, dressing the body involves actions undertaken to modify and supplement the body in order to address physical needs and to meet social and cultural expectations about how individuals should look. This process includes all five sense of seeing, touching, hearing, smelling, and tasting — regardless of the society and culture into which an individual is born. (Eicher et al. 2008: 4)

In addition to clothes, footwear is what separates human beings from animals as well. Generally speaking, animals do not wear shoes or sandals, which Eicher and her authors prefer to call "foot enclosures" (2008: 186) to avoid any ethnocentric or Eurocentric cultural biases which come with specific terminologies.

The first book dedicated entirely to shoes was *De Calceo Antiquo* written in Latin in 1667 by the breechmaker turned scholar Benoit Baudouin and Giulio Negrone, a Jesuit/instructor in rhetoric and theology (McNeil and Riello 2011b: 12). But, in contrast to research on clothes, there were less interests on footwear until quite recently. Margrethe Hald explains in her book *Primitive Shoes: An Archaeological-Ethnological Study Based upon Shoe Finds from the Jutland Peninsula* that footwear as a historical artifact has less appeal for research than clothing items:

> Danish shoe finds, being relatively few in number, merit attention all the more if they are to contribute to the widening of our knowledge of dress in Denmark in prehistoric times. But it must be admitted that worn and broken shoes are without charm. They have not the immediate appeal of many other impressive and well-preserved articles of clothing. Nor are they attractive an object to study. (Hald 1972: 7)

Some studies on footwear trace the history of shoes at different time periods. For instance, William (Boy) Habraken's heavily illustrated book on *Tribal and Ethnic Footwear of the World* (2000) tells stories of footwear from around the world. The book is based on the author's private collection of over 2,500 pairs of shoes collected from more than a 155 countries. It shows a long and deep history of footwear found in different regions of the world. Similarly, Hald's study (1972) starts from the fragments of Danish shoes from Bronze Age that looked like foot-wrappings that was excavated in 1935, which indicates how far back in history people were covering their feet. She studies the development of shoe construction up until the eleventh century providing us with diagrams and flat patterns of different shoe types from different regions at different time periods. But she provides little sociocultural meanings of these shoes. Both of these studies do not discuss the meanings behind the shoes and simply give descriptions of them.

Wilcox (1948) takes a look at footwear from cross-cultural perspectives and offers a cross-cultural overview of non-western footwear in Egypt, China, Korea, and Japan in addition to western footwear in different historical time periods, such as Medieval Europe, Renaissance, up until the twentieth century. Although she does not provide the source of historical evidence, it is a good start to understand footwear from the global perspective.

It is clear that footwear plays a meaningful role in human dress culture, and we can place footwear studies within fashion and dress studies as a subcategory. And just like clothes, footwear can be researched and analyzed from multidisciplinary approaches. June Swann writes:

Footwear has been essential to our way of life since man left the "Garden of Eden". It should no longer be associated with dirty streets, for the horse has long ceased to be our main form of transport. Shoes are exciting objects which reveal more about human nature than almost anything else. Although hitherto the history of shoes has tended to be a minor field of costume study, those who persist will truly find rich rewards. (2001: 10)

With the growth and development of professional scholarly research on fashion and dress, a thematic research focus is becoming increasingly segmented. Footwear used to be just a part of a research project on clothing fashion. Fortunately, in the past twenty to thirty years, we are seeing more research carried out on shoes, and more and more scholars have been taking up footwear as their primary research theme. In addition, in recent years, we see exhibitions and conferences dedicated to footwear.

For instance, in June 2015, the Victoria and Albert Museum in the UK opened an exhibition *Shoes: Pleasure and Pain* looking at the extremes of footwear collected from the world, and the Great North Museum in Newcastle, UK, is hosting an academic conference *Shoes, Slippers and Sandals: Feet and Footwear in Antiquity*. The Brooklyn Museum in New York also organized an exhibition in 2015 entitled *Killer Heels: The Art of The High-Heeled Shoe* exploring the history and the social significance of high-heeled shoes, followed by *The Rise of Sneaker Culture* exhibition which opened in July 2015 and was first shown at the Bata Shoe Museum in 2013. The Museum at the Fashion Institute of Technology (FIT) in New York hosted the *Shoe Obsession* exhibition in 2013 showcasing 150 pairs of contemporary footwear. In conjunction with the exhibition on shoes at the University of Northampton Museum, also in 2013, *The World at Your Feet*

Conference took place at the University. Its Museum has about 12,000 types of shoes collected from around the world.

The foot has been treated as part of the human body, and footwear can be studied as the clothed foot just like fashion is treated as a clothed body. As McNeil and Riello explain:

> Since the 1980s, postmodernism and minimalism have proposed new visions of fashion and the body. They have underlined the fragmentary nature of fashion. The international catwalk has been subjected to new ideas based on the "disintegration" of dress, unusual and clashing combinations, and the conception of the body as composed of single "body parts" or details, rather than as a figure or silhouette. (McNeil and Riello 2011b: 21)

Furthermore, we are seeing an increasing number of academic journals on fashion and dress studies, such as *Fashion Theory* edited by Valerie Steele, *Fashion Practice* edited by Sandy Black and Marilyn DeLong, *The International Journal of Fashion Studies* by Emanuela Mora, Agnès Rocamora, and Paolo Volonté. Other fashion-related journals are also becoming more segmented, such as *Critical Studies on Fashion and Beauty*, *Journal of Punk and Post-Punk* which includes topics on fashion, *Fashion, Style and Popular Culture*, *Clothing Cultures*, and *Critical Studies in Men's Fashion* among many others. We will probably see a peer-reviewed scholarly journal on footwear in the near future.

While scholars are sharing theoretical frameworks and methodological strategies in research, the object of research is becoming narrowly focused which would deepen the understanding of the subject. Riello explains the interdisciplinary nature of fashion studies (2006: 5): "The label 'fashion studies' has been invented to draw together scholars interested in dress and fashion who come from very different backgrounds ... the aim is to integrate history, material culture, literature, society and the economy."

Studies on historical footwear

As indicated earlier, research on footwear is often integrated into fashion and dress studies in general in which the primary discussions are based on clothing. It is assumed that there is more to say on clothing fashion than shoes fashion. Therefore, academic studies that pay attention only to footwear are limited. Costume and fashion historians examine western dress while adding shoes to their discussion. While footwear studies are limited, the scholars make an attempt to explore the sociocultural significance of shoes around the world. Shoes have gone beyond their protective functions. McNeil and Riello explain:

> Footwear is more than a simple wrapping or protection for the foot. The notion that indicate a great deal about a person's taste (or disdain for such things) and identity—national regional, professional—class status and gender, is not an invention of modernity. (McNeil and Riello 2011a: 3)

Different types, shapes, and forms of footwear can carry sociocultural and religious symbolism. They can be interpreted within their specific cultural context. In both western and non-western cultures, social hierarchy and social differences among people could be demonstrated through footwear, especially in cultures where barefoot is the norm, wearing a pair of shoes is a sign of status. As Swann writes:

> The history of shoe fashions when compared with the history of dress is, even now, sixty years later, still in its infancy. Few countries have published a comprehensive history of footwear of their country or regions, making study of variations difficult. The thirty or more shoes museums scattered around the world in Europe, Asia and the Americas, each persists in trying to tell the same fashion story, with few exploring in any depth the specialities of their own land or town. (Swann 2001: 8)

Swann (2001) conducted an expansive study of shoe constructions, patterns, and styles evolved in the three Scandinavian countries: Norway, Sweden, and Finland. She looks at the footwear in chronological order, beginning with a brief discussion of basic types which apply worldwide. She starts from prehistoric footwear and then moves on to the medieval period to the sixteenth century (Swann 2001).[1]

Some of the most striking footwear found in the western costume history is men's *poulaine* and women's *chopine*. *Poulaine* was footwear for men with long pointed toes, and it remained popular for about 150 years from the fourteenth to the mid-fifteenth century. The toe grew so long that it was attached to a chain or cord to keep the wearer from falling. Although they were later banned by church and state, the pointed shoe toes were once status symbols.

> From dated documents, art and archaeological evidence it is clear that pointed toes of two to five inches were very much in fashion during the late fourteenth century throughout Europe. The style subsided in around 1400 but was revived in the mid fifteenth century becoming even more popular than before. (Walford 2007: 12)

In addition, eroticism also lay behind the genesis of this elongated shoes. Lois Banner in her "The Fashionable Sex, 1100–1600" explains:

European folk belief categorized feet, like noses, as related to the penis, the size of one reflective of the size of the other. Thus at one point the fashion was that the extensions of the *poulaines* should be filled with saw-dust so that they would stand upright. And it was not unknown that some wearers of these shoes would shape and colour the extension to resemble a penis. In 1367 the French king, Charles V, prohibited the wearing of *poulaines* shaped like penises. (Banner 2008:10)

Studies on *poulaines* show that a gender-specific footwear appeared as early as the fourteenth century and also falsify our assumption that only female footwear was treated as an erotic object.

Moreover, between the fourteenth and sixteenth centuries, a new type of shoes called *chopines* was found in Italy and was popular especially among Venetian women. It has a practical protection function with thick platform soles designed to protect the foot from dirty streets. In addition, it also had an adornment and a status function for the wearer. Andrea Vianello conducted research on the Venetian *chopines* during the time of Renaissance in Europe (2011: 76–93). These thick soles were often made out of cork, and their height could be up to twenty inches tall (about 50 centimeters). Initially, *chopines* were adopted by both men and women, but their use by men were eventually forbidden and even fined for wearing them, since they were considered to be too feminine. By the early sixteenth century, they became an exclusively female footwear. Vianello (2011) explains that a diverse form of footwear had precise information about the wearer's status and identity, and even a few inches in the thickness of the soles seem to have originally revealed the distinction between the famous and the infamous, and between appropriate and inappropriate behavior.

In contrast to studies on western historical footwear, there are fewer studies on non-western historical footwear that are scholarly and have a unique regional focus. Marianne Hulsbosch's study on *Pointy Shoes and Pith Helmets: Dress and Identity Construction in Ambon from 1850 to 1942* (2014) is a valuable research on the sociocultural meanings of Ambonese dress and footwear through which their ethnic identities were constructed during Dutch colonial times. Ambon is one of many islands in Indonesia and was the headquarters of the Dutch East India Company between 1610 and 1619.

Christian Ambonese middle-class women, who were typically Eurasians or ethnic women with European status, were named Nona Cenela (literally translated as Mrs. Slippers) after their shoes, which were decorated toe slippers called "cenela" embodying the multiethnic history of the Ambonese. Their origin is believed to be Chinese because of the decoration, but those could also be Arabic due to the shape (Hulsbosch 2014: 54). The pointed toe is also reminiscent of the shoe that was popular in Europe during the Middle Ages. It was not a comfortable shoe to wear, so one needed some practice to walk in them. In Ambonese colonial society, the cenela was used as a way of enforcing and demonstrating women's leisurely status and signaled freedom. A woman wearing celena did not engage in manual labor. Hulsbosch explains the dichotomous elements of the shoe as follows:

> The cenela simultaneously conveys bondage and freedom, vulnerability and resilience. In one sense, the slipper is the ultimate symbol of subjugation; it severely limits physical mobility and reduces the wearer to a slow, deliberate walk. (Hulsbosch 2014: 55)

This footwear was clearly a status symbol to indicate one's high-ranking social position. Once the women became older, they wore a different type of slippers called Nyonya Kaus (literally translated as Mrs. Stocking). They were the ultimate symbol of maturity, wealth, and status. These slippers had blunt toes pointing straight up at a ninety-degree angle, and they did not allow the wearer to keep the shoe on the foot. One needed to have ultimate physical control to move in these slippers (Hulsbosch 2014: 56–57). Therefore, in the Ambonese culture, female footwear symbolized women's age, social status, and identity, and were as important as how they dressed.

Martha Chaiklin's article on "Purity, Pollution and Place in Traditional Japanese Footwear" is a major contribution to the study of Japanese historical footwear (2011: 160–180). Chaiklin analyzes the relationship between moral and physical cleanliness and daily life during Japan's Tokugawa period (1600–1868) and analyzes the role of footwear from commercial, production, and social/external perspectives. As in many other cultures around the world, footwear was reserved basically for higher classes, and it was not until the seventeenth century that footwear became common among commoners in Japan. Thonged footwear, such as *geta*, wooden sandals, or *zori*, made out of leather and more formal than *geta* and often worn with split-toed socks, was popular. There was a clear distinction between "polluted outdoor" and "pure indoor," and footwear was never worn inside a house. This is a Japanese custom which still remains today. Everyone takes off their shoes while entering a house because the outside ground is a source of uncleanliness literally and figuratively. The custom of removing one's shoes when entering a house used to exist in Ancient India as well, and it exists even today also (Jain-Neubauer 2000: 111).

As for the history of African footwear and dress before the twentieth century, Tunde M. Akinwumi writes in her "Interrogating Africa's Past: Footwear among the Yoruba" (2011) that they are difficult to investigate and therefore have been neglected. She studies the footwear tradition among the various social strata of the Yoruba society from the earliest times to the beginning of the twentieth century by foregrounding the sociopolitical and economic factors that impinged on it (Akinwumi 2011: 183). From the fifteenth century, Trans-Saharan trade became widespread, and traders in West Africa marketed various products including cheap and simple slippers and expensive embroidered sandals, and the environmental context of Yorubaland provided another strong motive for the Yoruba to "indigenize" clogs and other "foreign" footwear, and much of Yorubaland is covered by rain forest that produces various types of hardwoods such as mahogany, cedar, and obeche, suitable for wooden footwear (Akinwumi 2011:185). Similarly, Doran Ross (2011) also gives a brief account of African footwear and describes that traditional African leaders have long been identified with distinctive footwear, and among the most unusual are the raffia shoes (*mateemy manneemy*) worn by the kings of the Democratic Republic of Congo as part of the royal dress anywhere in Africa. Each toe is individually encased in its own sleeve, and the top of the footwear is often adorned with lines of cowry shells and blue and white beads, often in a distinctive guilloche pattern.

Footwear and sumptuary laws

Because of the social, economic, and political implications attached to shoes, many of the historical footwear found around the world were restricted and controlled by sumptuary laws which regulated people's expenditure on luxury items, including shoes. That is an indication that footwear was more than an item of dress with protective functions but was granted a certain amount of prestige and honor to a particular type of footwear, whether it was shape, height, or fabric.

Sumptuary laws on footwear existed in Europe as early as the fifteenth century. According to Walford's research:

> In 1463, England's Edward IV proclaimed, "No knight under the state of a lord, esquire gentlemen, nor other person shall use nor wear … any shoes or boots having pikes passing the length of two inches". This fashion crackdown was extended two years later to include everyone. A papal bill followed in 1468, which called the style "a scoffing against God and the church, a worldly vanity and a mad presumption" but neither royal edict nor papal bill dissuaded followers of the poulaine. A victim of its own success, the style only fell from favour when fashionable nobles abandoned long toes because they had become too common. By 1949 the style had all but disappeared. (Walford 2007: 12)

To what extent sumptuary laws were applicable or not is debatable, but it shows the trickle-down effect of fashion which the upper class wanted to stop. During the reign of Louis XIV (1643–1717), red-heeled shoes could only be worn by aristocrats at the king's court. By restricting colors and decorations, materials, and shapes to a chosen few, as part of sumptuary laws, shoes were symbols of power and status. Those who could not afford or were not allowed to buy a certain type of shoes wore wooden clogs which were much more economical and long-lasting than leather footwear (Roche 1997). There were also sumptuary laws for expensive shoes in Italy. There were eleven laws in northern Italy between 1512 and 1595, which forbade the use of gold, silver, and embroidery for shoes and especially for *chopines* (Vianello 2011).

In addition, sumptuary laws on footwear were also found in Asia and Africa. Zamperini, in an influential text of the Confucian canon, states that:

> People should take off their shoes before entering the house, that shoes and socks should be removed at banquet, and that ministers meeting with the emperor should also take off both shoes and socks. However bare feet were a taboo on occasions of ceremonial worship. Shoes of course, in China as well as in many other premodern societies could show the social status of the wearer, and throughout time complex rules and sumptuary laws developed to ensure that certain colors of shoe-wear remained the privilege of the wealthy and the powerful. (Zamperini 2011: 200)

Similarly, in early modern Japan with a rigid social structure based on modified Confucian ideas, footwear was as much an indication of social class as clothing, and challenges to that order were frowned upon (Chaiklin 2011). The warrior class ranked at the top followed by the farmer, the artisan, and the merchant at the bottom. Outcastes in Japan during the Edo period (1603–1868) were only allowed to wear straw sandals and *seta* which is a type of sandal made of bamboo bark with leather soles that developed around the end of the sixteenth century and came to be closely associated with, but not exclusive to, outcastes (Chaiklin 2011: 173).

In Africa, Akinwumi explains that footwear not worn by common people was reserved for important men, and the lower strata of society were excluded from wearing any kind of footwear until the early decades of the twentieth century.

> An association between the use footwear and regal status meant that even nobles could be refused permission to use footwear. When an oba (a king in the Yoruba language) wore clogs, his people perceived him as symbolically walking on a dais. The clog, which was about six inches or more high, exaggerated the oba's height, and metaphorically elevated him to the highest position and status in society. (Akinwumi 2011: 191)

The arrival of westerners gradually forced the royalty which affected the custom of appearing barefoot in front of the king. Both the educated elite and the visiting European missionaries called for an end to the practice, and commoners were eventually allowed to wear shoes in the palace. This was seen as the ultimate sign of defeat, as one of the strongest sartorial prerogatives of kingship had come to an end (Akinwumi 2011: 194).

Footwear in rituals and religion

Shoes fulfill significant roles in the world's major and minor religions, such as Christianity, Islam, Hinduism, and Judaism among others, both in the past and present. Religious dress, including footwear, follows their code which the leaders and followers are required to abide by. Lynne Hume's study on religious dress includes several important accounts on footwear (2013). She writes:

> Religious dress is a visible signifier of difference. The message communicated is that the wearer chooses to follow a certain set of ideological or religious principles and practices. Dress distinctions function to set one religious community apart from other religious communities, and they also operate within a religion to distinguish hierarchies, power structures, gender distinctions, ideas of modesty, roles, mores, group identity and belief and ideology. (Hume 2013: 1)

Islam considers the body, including feet, as a gift from God, but it is also a potential source of shame for men and women and therefore needs to be concealed and covered. When one enters the mosque, footwear must be removed on entering in case ritually impure substances have adhered to the sole of the shoe, a rule which also applies to entering a graveyard (Hume 2013: 64). Consequently, shoes are designed in a way that they can be easily removed. While footwear is for a physical protection, it can also be a psychological protection as Doran Ross (2011) explains: "In their most fundamental senses, soled footwear obviously serve physically and materially protective functions, but many of the various forms of footwear discussed here also serve as protective amulets and charms. Some of these function under the tenets of Islam, where images of the sandals of the Prophet Mohammed are a recurring design motif in jewelry, leatherwork, and even carved wood doors."

In Judaism, men and women must dress modestly and show as little skin as possible. Much of people's dress in the Hasidic community is based on their movement that began in the eighteenth century in Eastern Europe. The Hasidic top-ranking leaders, the rebbes, follow the strict men's dress code. They are the only ones who wear the shich and zocken which are slipper-like shoes and white knee socks (Ouaknin 2000: 114). Shoes are also used in religious rituals. According to a Judaic rite, an unmarried brother-in-law of a childless widow is obliged to marry her, but the widow can release him from this obligations by publicly removing a ritual halizah shoe (which dates back to about 1900) from his foot; he is then free to marry somebody else (Nahshon 2008). "Shoes have become a metonym for the victims of the Holocaust, their footwear and other personal effects collected by the Nazi killing machine…" (Nahshon 2008: 1). Shoes are a metaphor for wandering and journey.

According to Beer (2004: 227), an ordained Buddhist monk hardly ever wore shoes, but when they did, they wore simple wooden or leather sandals or thongs for the protection purposes. Like in Islam, shoes are always removed at the entrance of any Buddhist temple since they are regarded as a dirty part of the body. From the monastic rules prescribed for Buddhist monks is the custom of not wearing shoes in the presence of elders, or superior monks, or the Master (Jain-Neubauer 2000: 115). According to an ordained Buddhist nun, Venerable Lhundub Tendron, who was ordained in 2012 said (in Hume 2013: 115): "you put the robe on over your head; you do not step into it and you don't put your robe on the ground; this would be disrespectful."

Buddhism started in India and has spread to other parts of the world, such as China, Tibet, Mongolia, Cambodia, Japan, Korea, and Sri Lanka among many others. As it spread, the form, color, and choice of fabric for the robe adapted according to region, culture, climate, and the particular section, tradition, or school of Buddhism and the lineage of the wearer (Hume 2013: 109–110). For example, Buddhist dress in Tibet including footwear is elaborate and colorful. According to Desideri (2010: 328), they wear boots that reach to the knees both indoors and outdoors, and the part that covers the foot is made of well-tanned white leather, and from the foot to the knees, it is made of red cloth ornamented with beautiful silk and embroidery work.

In Christianity, the leaders have historically followed the tight dress code. A medieval pope wore red stockings and red shoes with a white linen robe and a red or white cloak called a papal mantle, and red stockings (Hume 2013: 17). Pope Pius VII, Roman Catholic Pontiff from 1800 to 1823, wore these custom-made red velvet shoes with gold embroidery and cruciform motif (McIver 1994). The shoes worn by popes are often adorned with symbols and motifs that relate specifically to a pope's position as head of the Roman Catholic Church which symbolizes his ecclesiastical status.

Hume analyzes the life and dress of Amish people whose fundamental life philosophy is based on "humility, simplicity, equality and orderliness" (Hume 2013: 38), as they abide by their Ordnung. In addition to their strict dress code, there were rules about shoes. Garret explains in her autobiographical essay that in her community, they were to be laced-up and wear black leather shoes coupled with thick, knee-high nylon leggings (Garret and Garret 2003: 13). Women wear flat dress shoes that are plain and black, and no high heels are permitted (Hume 2013: 39). Their dress styles indicate that they are always ready to work.

In her *Feet & Footwear in Indian Culture* (2000), Jain-Neubauer offers the historical outline of footwear in India from ancient times (since 4000 BC), and also explains the deep cultural meanings of feet, footwear, and ornaments using literary and archaeological sources. In Indian culture which consists of Hinduism, Buddhism, and Jainism, the shoe is a symbolic representation of the deity. Paduka, toe-knob sandals, is a wooden board cut roughly in the shape of a footprint with a post and a knob at the front which is held between the big and the second toe. This footwear is associated with a holy man, sacred person, and a religious teacher who wanders from village to village, and it indicates a religious status.

The ascetics of the Hindu, Buddhist and Jaina sects were not generally permitted the worldly luxury of footwear, but to prevent contact with any ritually impure substances they were allowed to use footwear made from wood or other such "pure" materials. Footwear of divine personages were the vehicles of the dust of their holy feet and as such was considered to be worthy of veneration. This idea led to the practice of worshipping holy men and divinities not in the form of their anthropomorphic image but by their symbolic representation in the form of the footwear. (Jain-Neubauer 2000: 14–15)

Footwear as a fetish object

Footwear is a gendered object which clearly distinguishes a male shoe from a female shoe. There was a transformation of meanings attached to high heels which used to be worn by both men and women, and now it is exclusively a female footwear. Much emphasis on footwear research has been on female shoes, high heels in particular, since it has a great deal of sexual appeal. It is not only the footwear but also women's ankles, bare feet, and small feet that are treated as a fetish object (see Conclusion Chapter).

Today, the different shapes and colors of men's and women's shoes revolve primarily around the construction of gender difference. It will be argued that many of these gendered distinctions developed in the so-called long eighteenth century (McNeil and Riello 2011c: 95). By the early seventeenth century, upper-class men wore high heels, but by the mid-eighteenth century, men stopped wearing them, and high heels became exclusively female-gendered footwear (Small 2014: 9). As men's fashion became more subdued during the late eighteenth and nineteenth centuries, high heels were increasingly associated with femininity, fetishism, and eroticism as men had abandoned adornment and fashion.

Corsets, women's underwear, and high-heeled shoes have been treated as fetish objects. Valerie Steele[2] makes an analogy between corsets and high heels both of which eroticize the body:

> They arch the foot and put the legs in a state of tension resembling that of sexual arousal. High heels change not only the wearer's stance, but also her walk-making her totter, wiggle, or sway. High-heeled shoes, especially those with tapered heels and pointed toes, also make a woman's feet look smaller. (Steele 2012: 8)

The topic of female fetish objects has been a fascination for many writers. David Kunzle published a book entitled *Fashion & Fetishism* (2004) in which he talks about fetish objects, including corsets and high heels, and about the hierarchical symbolism of different shapes of one's foot. The big-spayed-toe foot has been generally regarded as "low". Lisa Small in *the Killer Heels: The Art of the High-Heeled Shoe* exhibition catalogue writes (2014: 9): "High heels and other elevated shoes have been status symbols for centuries. Coveted, adored, reviled, regulated, mocked, fetishized, and legislated against, they have also been central to the construction and performance of femininity." Caroline Weber in her article "The Eternal High Heel: Eroticism and Empowerment" (2014: 15–23) discusses the history of high-heeled footwear. Steele explores fashion as a symbolic system linked to the expressions of sexuality—both sexual behavior (including erotic attraction) and gender identity (1996: 4). She points out that fetishism is not only "about" sexuality but also very much about power and perception.

> The concept of fetishism has recently assumed a growing importance in critical thinking about the cultural construction of sexuality. Works such as Fetishism as Cultural Discourse and Feminizing the Fetish complement or critique the voluminous clinical literature on fetishism as a sexual "perversion." Neo-Marxists analyze "commodity fetishism," feminist scholars explore the contested issues of "female fetishism," and art theorists stress the subversive role of fetishism in contemporary art, arguing that a fetish can be any article that shocks our sensibilities. (Steele 1996: 6)

Steele argues that fetishism is universal, and even if not, it has existed for thousands of years in many cultures while others argue that fetishism developed only in modern western society (1996: 21–22). She convincingly writes that fetishism is not an innate human behavior but a socially constructed one:

> There are cultural and historical reasons why certain items of clothing are often chosen as fetishes. High heels are strongly associated in our culture with a certain kind of fashionable and sexually sophisticated woman, which is why they are favored by prostitutes and cross-dressers .... Many characteristics commonly associated with feminine sexual attractiveness are accentuated by high-heeled shoes, which affect the wearer's gait and posture. By putting

the lower part of the body in a state of tension, the movement of the hips and buttocks is emphasized and the back is arched, thrusting the bosom forward. High heels also change the apparent contour of the legs, increasing the curve of the calf and tilting the ankle and foot forward, thus creating an alluringly long-legged look. Seen from a certain angle, a high-heeled shoe also recalls the female public triangle. (Steele 2011: 269)

In addition, Willaim A. Rossi in *The Sex Life of the Foot and Shoe* (1976) makes a psychoanalytical connection between sex and footwear, and he associates female footwear with sexual desire. Not simply the shoes, but shoe ornaments were originally genital symbols, and large buttons symbolized testicles, and the fur trimming around the shoe's collar represented pubic hair (Rossi 1976: 222–223). Today, these items have lost their phallic symbolism for most people.

In "A Delicate Balance: Women, Power and High Heels," Elizabeth Semmelhack chronologically addresses the history of women's high heels and explains how its popularity had fluctuated over the centuries (2011: 224–247). The high heel's association with social status continued through the latter half of the seventeenth century, but gender distinctions became increasingly evident, and men's heels were sturdy or blocky while women's heels were more tapered and delicate in design, reflecting the cultural preference for a dainty female foot (Semmelhack 2011: 225). By the early eighteenth century, the footwear became an exclusively feminine form of footwear, and gender is now clearly marked in footwear, and the higher the heel, the greater is the shoe's association with female sexuality (Semmelhack 2011: 225; Steele 2012: 10). Its popularity subsides around 1780s but remerges in the middle of the nineteenth century for wealthy, privileged women. Semmelhack explains the sexual implications and power of high heels as follows:

In the second half of the nineteenth century, the presence and the idea of the courtesan and sexual commodification became central to European intellectual and artistic thought. The concept of the courtesan linked female "power" and sexual manipulation. It also illustrated the failure of female agency and provided a warning to those "respectable" women who sought more autonomy …. the commodification of female sexuality became a mainstay of modernity and defined sexual allure was emerging as a goal of fashion. High heels, in particular, became infused with erotic significance. (Semmelhack 2011: 230)

By this time, men were no longer wearing high heels, and they became part of women's dress. High heels are eroticized and sexualized, and the higher the heel, the greater the shoe's association with sexuality (Semmelhack 2011: 233). There was a clear cultural connection between the height of shoes and a woman's moral character, which continued throughout the sixteenth century. Column-like *chopines* were emblematic of sexual availability and were associated with courtesans. This is comparable to a pair of high platform clogs worn by a Japanese courtesan, *Oiran*, in the seventeenth century. Both of them restrict women's mobility but could also be a symbol of social status.

Conclusion

By placing footwear within fashion and dress studies and reviewing studies on historical and contemporary footwear in the West and non-West, we see that, like clothing, it has adornment and status functions in addition to protective functions. Shoes are more than a tangible object that covers our feet for practical purposes. They have multilayered social, cultural, religious, political, and legal meanings, as discussed in this chapter. As we convey a great deal of social information about ourselves through clothing and dress, our shoes are also able to transmit information about our social class, status, religion, sexuality, and occupation, among many others.

2

SNEAKERS AS A SUBCULTURE: EMERGING FROM UNDERGROUND TO UPPERGROUND

A review of the literature on footwear studies, which mostly focuses on historical shoes, offers us some insights into sneakers. It shows that studies on contemporary shoes, especially on men's shoes, are limited and that there are no groups of people who are united by one type of shoes and who can be called a subculture.

Subcultural theorists find the pattern, tendency, and commonalities across different subcultural groups as a community and among the members of that community. In that way, we can begin to make a theoretical interpretation about subcultures in general. In order to investigate a subculture as a social group as well as an agent of male socialization, we can focus on their social communications where meanings are negotiated through dialogues and interactions. We must be careful not to be monolithic about subcultures because they produce different interpretations around themselves as individuals and as a collective group. While many do share similarities and commonalities, no two subcultures are identical.

In this chapter, I treat a community of sneaker enthusiasts as a subcultural group and explore to what extent it can be explained by various social theories including subcultural theories. Sneaker enthusiasts call themselves "sneakerheads," "sneakerholics," or "sneaker pimps." A group that is formed by and with sneaker fans and collectors can be another case study in subcultural studies since they share many, but not all, of the determinants and variables that other youth subcultures consist of. At the same time, they are also unique in that they are bounded by one object, that is, sneakers. They worship and celebrate sneakers as an object of desire, which contain a great deal of social information.

Subcultures can be constructed around any beliefs, attitudes, interests, or activities. Every subculture has its own values and norms that the participants share, and that gives them a common group or organizational identity. Wearing the right pair of sneakers, however it is defined, gives them a title of "a true sneakerhead."

The sneaker subculture that originally emerged from a hip-hop culture which emerged from a street-produced community uses their own language, and they have their own verbal communication methods, using distinct jargon, phrases, slangs, and idioms to explain various types and sneakers which outsiders would not understand (see Table 2.1).

Table 2.1 *Sneaker Glossary and Commonly Used Abbreviations*

Abbreviation	Terminology
3M	Reflective Material
ACG	All Conditions Gear
AF1	Air Force 1
AJ	Air Jordan
AM	Air Max
AZG	Air Zoom Generation
B-Grade	A shoe that is produced in the factory that may or may not have flaws. A certain amount has to be marked as "B-Grade" even if nothing is wrong with the shoe and usually found in outlet stores.
Beater	A shoe that is worn without care, usually a shoe that you wear all the time. This is also the same shoe you do not mind getting stepped on, scuffed, or dirty.
Bred	Black/Red Air Jordan colorway
BRS	Blue Ribbon Sports
Camo	Camouflage
CG	Cool Grey, usually used when talking about the Air Jordan III, IV, IX, or XI.
CO.JP	Concept Japan
DMP	Defining Moments Pack
DQM	Dave's Quality Meat (a shoe shop in NYC)
DS	Dead stock
DT	Diamond Turf

Abbreviation	Terminology
FT	Feng Tay (Nike Factory in Asia) usually seen on the box tag of sample or promo shoe.
G.O.A.T.	Greatest of All Time
GR	General Release
GS	Grade School
Heat	Hard to find shoes usually older models but can also be newer models.
HOA	History of Air
Holy Grail	Your most wanted shoe that may be very expensive or extremely rare.
HTM	A set of shoes designed by Hiroshi Fujiwara, Tinker Hatfield, and Mark Parker. HTM is the first letter of each designer's name.
Hyperstrike	Ultra limited and available at Nike shops with a Tier 0 and 1 account. Not many shops have these accounts because they are very hard to get. Also, some people may call shoes numbered at 500 pairs or less a "Hyperstrike".
ID	Individually Designed
ISS	Instyleshoes.com (Forum)
J's	Jordans
JB	Jordan Brand
LBJ	Lebron James
LE	Limited Edition
LS	Lifestyle which is a Jordan product that is usually associated with matching clothing and is geared toward trendy fashion than toward athletic performance.
NDS	Near dead stock
NIB	New in Box
NL	No Liner
NSB	Nikeskateboarding.org (Forum)
NT	Nike Talk (Forum)
NWT	New with Tags
OG	Original

Abbreviation	Terminology
P-Rod	Paul Rodriquez (a skater for Nike with a signature shoe line)
PE	Player Exclusive
Premium	Usually made with high-quality construction or material and will most likely cost more
Quickstrike	Only released at special Nike account stores, in most cases may pop out of no where in limited numbers
Retro	Re-Release
Retro +	Not an original Jordan colorway
SB	Skateboard
SBTG	Sabotage (the world famous custom designer)
SE	Special Edition
SVSM	Saint Vincent Saint Mary (Lebron James' High School)
UNDFTD	Undefeated (a shoe shop in Los Angeles, CA)
Uptowns	Air Force 1
VNDS	Very near dead stock
X	Usually stands for "and".

Based on information sourced from "A Beginner's Guide to Sneaker Terminology", a list compiled by Nick Engvall, Brandon Edler and Russ Bengtson (http://www.complex.com/sneakers/2012/09/a-beginners-guide-to-sneaker-terminology/) and Sneaker Slang Glossary (http://osneaker.com/glossary.html)

There is a great deal of influential and important subcultural studies that have come out of the United States and the United Kingdom focusing on specific social groups that distinguish themselves from the so-called mainstream society. The Chicago School which refers to the Sociology Department at the University of Chicago produced major research studies in urban sociology using ethnographic fieldwork as a research method, and they made a major contribution to the development of a micro-level social theory, symbolic interactionism, in explaining marginal groups of people. As early as 1918, W.I. Thomas and Florian Witold Znaniecki published their book on Chicago's Polish immigrants (1918); Nels Anderson wrote a book on *The Hobo* (1922) which was about homelessness in Chicago; Frederic Thrasher's study was on gangs that breed in a particular neighborhood (1927); Edward Franklin Frazer's work was on *The Negro Family in the United States* (1939). Their research subjects were often poor immigrants and racial minorities who were detached from the mainstream, or the deviant groups such as homeless people or gang members, many of whom lived on the social periphery.[1] It was not until the 1940s that the term "subculture" was beginning to be used to account for particular kinds of social difference in a pluralized and fractured United States (Gelder 2005: 21).

In contrast, the Centre for Contemporary Cultural Studies (CCCS) at the University of Birmingham, UK, established in 1964, paid attention to the Marxist concept of social class as their central theme in reference to the emergence of subcultures, youth subcultures in particular. The researchers at CCCS explicitly state that subculture is essentially a working-class phenomenon. Based on this idea, if one belongs to an elite class, there is no need for him or her to be a member of a subculture. The two most important books that were published by the CCCS scholars are *Resistance through Rituals* (1976) edited by Stuart Hall and Tony Jefferson and *Subculture: The Meaning of Style* by Dick Hebdige (1979). They examined skinheads, mods, and teddy boys (Hall and Jefferson 1976), and punks (Hebdige 1979), all of which have distinct stylistic expressions. In terms of their methodological research strategies, they moved away from ethnography and applied semiotics in their analysis of youth subcultures.[2]

Clark explains the definition of subculture mainly includes young people:

It [subculture] has come to signify the twentieth-century category for youth groups who possess some sort of marked style and shared affiliations. Whereas sociologists use the term to describe an infinitely wider array of groups—sport fishermen, West Texas Baptists, or toy train hobbyists— "subculture" is more popularly used to characterize groups of young people. (Clark 2003: 223, footnote 2)

These two traditions in the United States and the United Kingdom have laid the foundation of all the subcultural studies that emerged afterward. In both of them, subcultures exist in opposition to mainstream and dominant culture, although the degree of resistance may vary from community to community.

However, recent scholars move beyond these traditions. As Bennet and Hodkinson explain:

This interpretation is out of step with research emerging from the field of youth transitions, in which a range of theorists have drawn attention to the apparently increasing diversity, complexity and longevity of youth and the porous nature of the boundaries between adolescence and adulthood. (2012: 1)

Post-subcultural theorists see limitations of the traditional understanding of subcultures, especially the CCCS framework (Bennett and Kahn-Harris 2004; Hodkinson 2002; Muggleton and Weinzierl 2003) because their approach with a focus on class tended to be age-specific and age-limited examining only people in teens and early twenties (Muggleton and Wienzierl 2003). Instead of the term "subculture," many post-subcultural theorists find it more appropriate to use the term "scene" proposed by Bennett and Peterson (2004). Bennett (2006: 223) points out that the concept portrays individuals as more reflexive in their appropriation and use of particular musical and stylistics resources. It also does not presume that all of a participant's actions are governed by subcultural standards (Bennett and Peterson 2004: 3). The relationship between style, musical taste, and identity has become progressively weaker and articulated more fluidity (Bennett and Kahn-Harris 2004: 11).

My research on sneakers is both empirical and theoretical, and I lean more toward the CCCS in placing sneaker enthusiasts within a sociological framework while reading the meanings of sneakers as a text but at the same time incorporating ethnography and face-to-face interactions with sneaker enthusiasts. Unlike post-subcultural theorists, I prefer to use the term "subculture" in my exploration of the sneaker community because I wish to show the disappearance of the underground and the hidden nature of a subculture and the emergence of an "upperground" subculture implying the social exposure of the community as the result of commodification. Unlike other contemporary youth groups, sneaker enthusiasts do not temporarily take part in a "scene." Sneaker fans almost never part with sneakers and are constantly with them. Their involvement in and commitment to the sneaker world is not transient, and that is manifested through their shoes.

I have conducted fieldwork attending sneaker events and conventions where sneaker collectors buy and sell their sneakers. At the same time, I have paid attention to different types of sneakers that they wear, observing how they are worn, what each type indicates, and what it means to be the insider members. Youth subcultures are becoming so complex and diversified that it is not just about a subculture versus a mainstream culture which is too simplistic a classification. As Weinzierl and Muggleton explain:

> The subculture concept seems to be little more than a cliché, with its implications that both "subculture" and the parent culture against which it is defined are coherent and homogenous formations that can be clearly demarcated. But contemporary youth cultures are characterized by far more complex stratifications than the suggested by the simple dichotomy of "monolithic mainstream"—"resistant subcultures". (Muggleton and Weinzierl 2003: 7)

I argue that there is an "underground subculture" and an "upperground subculture," and the sneaker subculture that used to be underground is now on the upperground and becoming increasingly apolitical, although it is still labeled as a subculture. As Weinzierl and Muggleton further point out:

> Certain contemporary "subcultural" movements can still express political orientation, the potential for style itself to resist appears largely lost, with any

"intrinsically" subversive quality to subcultures exposed as an illusion. Thus, while the analysis of the CCCS can still be regarded as pioneering scientific work, they no longer appear to reflect the political, cultural and economic realities of the twenty-first century. (Muggleton and Weinzierl 2003: 4)

Three waves of the sneaker phenomenon

I broadly classify a phenomenon of the sneaker collection and popularity into three periods and name them as different stages of "waves" borrowing the concept of different stages and waves that feminism has gone through:[3]

1) The First Wave Sneaker Phenomenon: This occurred locally in New York in the 1970s, and it is the pre-Jordan era which is prior to the introduction of Nike Air Jordan sneakers. This was the beginning of an underground sneaker subculture with the growth of hip-hop culture. The sneaker subculture was considered a hidden community that originally came out of the poor neighborhoods dominated mostly by racial minorities.

2) The Second Wave Sneaker Phenomenon: This is the post-Jordan era that started with the launch of the Nike Air Jordan sneakers which were produced in 1984 and released to the market in 1985. It was named after legendary American basketball player Michael Jordan. The post-Jordan era is the start of the commodification and the massification of sneakers which were intensified year after year. The sneaker phenomenon spread further and more widely to the world while gradually transcending cultural, racial, class, and national boundaries. It is no longer as underground or hidden as it used to be, although it is still a subculture. I would call it an "upperground subculture," which is a subculture that has appeared on the social surface and has become recognizable by the masses.

3) The Third Wave Sneaker Phenomenon: This began with the advent of the Internet and the development of smartphones and tablets in the twenty-first century in the West, American society in particular. We see the global spread and diffusion of the sneaker popularity in the fragmented postmodern age with an increasing usage of the social media as a communication tool. The new technological trend drastically transformed the sneaker enthusiasts' communication process and competition in speed. The trend that started during the Second Wave is now accelerated at a more rapid speed.

These three waves of the sneaker phenomenon are explored in-depth in this chapter as well as in the subsequent chapters.

The First Wave pre-Jordan Phenomenon as an underground subculture

To understand where a sneaker subculture started from and why, we must put sneakers within a larger historical framework of hip-hop which is of African American cultural aesthetic traditions and movements (Chang 2005, 2006; Price 2006; Rabaka 2011). A youth subculture is about a lifestyle which includes their preferences for music, books, arts, and fashion among others. Typical sneaker enthusiasts share a similar lifestyle, wearing jeans, a T-shirt, a baseball cap, favoring street art, such as graffiti, and listening to rap music. Sneakers were very much part of the music scene that originated in the African American community in New York.

In order for us to understand the origin of a sneaker subculture, we need to know about a hip-hop culture which is male-dominant, and in order to understand the origin of the hip-hop culture, we need to trace back the economic and social situations of New York City in the 1970s. Material objects, including dress and sneakers, are never independent of their social and cultural contexts and surroundings. The way we dress is consciously and subconsciously imposed on us by external factors. As long as something or someone belongs to a society, social influences are unavoidable.

The First Wave Sneaker Phenomenon has roots in the South Bronx, NY, which was the most impoverished neighborhood in the 1970s, and it was probably the worst times in the history of New York. This was when the city officially declared bankruptcy which led to the deterioration of people's living standards and the increase in the number of homeless people. The economy declined, the poverty rate soared along with the increasing crime rates in mugging, killing, drug dealing, and prostitution, among others. New York with a tarnished image was an extremely dangerous place to visit or live in. People lost jobs and were forced to live below their means. As a result, "Street gangs marked walls in local neighbor hoods to claim their territory, then individuals began spraying their names on the subways" (Aheran 2003: 20). At the time, there was a strong correlation between race and class since the majority of the poverty-stricken households were racial minorities, especially the black families. Unlike the recent decades where people celebrate and encourage diversity, racial pluralism, and multiculturalism, race was a class problem, and class was a race problem in the United States, and the city was clearly racially and socially divided.

Hip-hop culture and rap music, as a completely new music genre, were born under these circumstances. As DJ Kool Herc, who is known as the founding father of hip-hop, says (in Chang 2005: xiii): "Hip-hop is a family....This culture was born in the ghetto," and it was the solution to many of the social problems that the black people were facing. At the time, there was a political agenda in the hip-hop community that was definitely anti-mainstream. Price also explains:

> Hip hop was … the product of self-determination, self-realization, creativity an pride … . Former gang territories became prime locations for block parties and outdoor jams. Prior gang warfare turned into aggressive competitions or turntable jousting by DJs, joined by countless male and female street dancers, often called "b-boys" and "b-girls," and the colorful artistic presentations of graffiti artists. (Price 2006: xi)

DJ Kool Herc explains how it all started:

> When I started DJing back in the early '70s, it was just something that we were doing for fun. I came from "the people's choice," from the street. If the people like you, they will support you and your work will speak for itself. The parties I gave happened to catch on. They became a rite of passage for young people in the Bronx … . To me, hip-hop says, "Come as you are." We are a family. It ain't about security. It ain't about bling bling. It ain't about how much your gun can shoot. It ain't about $200 sneakers. It is not about me being better than you or you being better than me. It's about you and me, connecting one to one. That's why it has universal appeal … . It brings white kids together with Black kids, brown kids with yellow kids. (DJ Kool Herc in Chang 2005: xi)

Aheran explains how DJ Kool Herc and this new type of music culture attracted different members who all made a major contribution to the start of the culture:

> DJ Kool Herc, wanting to excite his b-boy dancers, developed technique in the mid-1970s of looping the drum break of a James Brown record, or other selections, to create a super hot, new percussive sound. DJ Afrika Bambaataa transformed the huge Blade Spades gang into The Mighty Zulu Nation centred around DJ parties and afrocentric cultural events. Grand Master Flash experimented with perfecting his cutting techniques and invited his b-boy squad to try flexing their style on the mic, which led to the formation of the Furious MC's. Hip-Hop was born. (Aheran 2003: 20–21)

It became extremely popular among the black youngsters who experienced poverty and racial injustice on a daily basis, and they had no motivations or dreams in American society where there was not enough affordable housing, adequate health care, decent employment, and high-quality education available to them. Hip-hop gave them an alternative and exciting lifestyle that was distinct and different from the mainstream White culture which was inaccessible and unreachable to them.

Sneaker fashion as hip-hop aesthetics from the street

Therefore, hip-hop is a not just a music genre but a culture by itself, and that includes a particular type of style. There are four foundational elements in hip-hop culture: DJing, graffiti, b-boying, and MCing, and each serves as a method of self-expression, and each intersects with the prevalence of gangs and the gang lifestyle during the 1960s (Price 2006: 21). Then the widespread popularity of the culture offered other opportunities for other elements to spread, such as fashion and language, all of which are part of hip-hop aesthetic (Price 2006: 21).

Danny Hoch (in Chang 2006: 349) investigated hip-hop aesthetics in graffiti, DJ, b-boy, and rap. He does not include clothing and footwear, but we can add sneakers to them since they have been an integral part of hip-hop aesthetics, and that is the reason why rap musicians almost always wear sneakers, and their fans and followers pay attention to them. While hip-hop was never viewed as legitimate "art," it has changed over the years.

In Jeff Chang's interview, DOZE, a b-boy and a graffiti artist says (Chang 2006: 321–330):

When you're talking about hip-hop, when you want to get a broader sense of the world, you're talking about poor people. Cause most of the fashion comes from the street- and who's the street? Usually working-class people who create style in fashion. So would that be hip-hop, or would that be urban influence? It has to do with poor people .... It has to do with a person who got creative and couldn't afford f*cking Bally's and created his own designer label on his pants, or cut his shirt in a certain way, or her shirt in a certain way, or tied it up in little knots. Because she couldn't afford to buy haute-culture top, she made her own. That's what hip-hop is in fashion: people creating what they like, creating the look. People used to pain on clothes, not go to the store and get something painted. They do it themselves. It's not authentic when you buy it off a shelf. It's just not. (DOZE in Chang 2006: 328–329)

Similarly, there is a strong correlation between hip-hop and street. Vogel also explains the meaning of "street" and "streetwear" which sneakers are a part of:

There is no formula to make something "street" ... streetwear is a combination of attitudes, aesthetics and activities that binds a group of people with similar interests together. It isn't something that can be analyzed from the outside, learned, reproduced and then packaged to be sold to the undeserving public. In order to be successfully involved in the streetwear industry, many would argue, including myself, that it is essential to have been a part of the subculture in the first place. (Vogel 2007: 8–9)

It is not an exaggeration to say that sneakers have been a part of rap musicians' uniform or their dress code in the past and today. Those who claimed that they were part of this group always wore sneakers which were an important part of their style and identity. Since hip-hop is directly correlated to a black culture, sneakers were associated with black people, especially during the pre-Jordan era.

> The mid-1970s saw the emergence of hip-hop culture, and with it a new-found attitude to the wearing of sneakers ... . Sneakers were now being preserved in pristine condition for that all-important fresh-out-of the box look- and rising prices also ensured that looking after your sneakers guaranteed getting your money's worth. This trend was seen the world over; whether sneakers were initially worn for skateboarding, playing football or just wandering the streets, it was hip-hop culture that turned them into objects of desire. Just think back to Run-DMC's "Walk This Way" promo; it's a much-cited example, but those box-fresh adidas Superstars had a lasting impact on the youth culture of the day. (Intercity 2008: 6)

Individuals, especially the lost youths, may have higher chances of joining marginal groups due to their dissatisfaction and discontent about their lives when they do not see anything positive about their future. There is no way they can achieve what the elites can, in terms of wealth, prestige, and power, and it may result in forming an underground subculture with its own value system, and a group of sneaker enthusiasts in the 1970s may largely fit into this model. Joining a subcultural community gives them an option to receive the recognition, attention, and respect that they could not otherwise receive. The participation in subcultures may come from their hopeless social environment, and these factors lead youths to create their own versions of aesthetics which may appear to be deviant from the mainstream perspective. Subcultural membership provides a physical, virtual, and symbolic space to those who feel that they are marginal.

Rejection of a legitimate aesthetic taste

Therefore, the First Wave Sneaker Phenomenon was the outcome of the young minority youths resisting against the mainstream American society, and it was mostly dominated by racial minorities. Bobbito Garcia, a sneaker connoisseur, said to me explicitly in a phone interview: "Sneaker subculture came out of the people of color."

Ken Gelder defines subcultures as groups of people that are in some way represented as nonnormative and/or marginal through their particular interests and practice, through what they are, what they do, and where they do it (2005: 1).[4] He explained that subcultures are social with their own shared conventions, values, and rituals. He described different forms and practices of subculture and explained that the members' negative relations to work and class; a specific geographical territory, such as the street, the hood, and the club, and excessive exaggerated stylistic expressions are some of the identifying points of a subcultural participation (Gelder 2007).

In the 1970s, fashion was synonymous with European luxury brands, such as a French Haute Couture dress or a tailor-made Savile Row business suit which most of the youngsters in the South Bronx had no access to and which they would have resisted, and a style that was functional used to have no place in fashion. But just like the punks, they created their own definition of fashion and aesthetics. The practice of sneaker painting and decoration, which still continues today, came out of the streets during the First Wave Sneaker Phenomenon (Plates 2.1 and 2.2). There was no institutional participation in promoting it as a trend or fashion. As Haenfler points out, a subculture as a social subgroup is distinguishable from mainstream culture by its nonnormative values, beliefs, symbols, and activities, and often, in the case of youth, styles and music (Haenfler 2014: 3).

Sneakers, especially during the pre-Jordan era, were never considered as mainstream fashion or a type of footwear with aesthetic function, but among the enthusiasts, they knew precisely which sneakers were considered a good taste. As time went on, sneakers were worn for adornment purposes, which will be elaborated in Chapters 3 and 4.

In the earlier studies of youth subcultures, deviance and resistance were the key concepts. They formed a subculture to go against the conventional society and thus marginalized themselves as a deviant group that resisted the dominant culture. There are different pieces and elements in a society, and each has its own function to make a whole. This is how social order becomes intact. But there are those who cannot achieve the society's conventional cultural goal through conventional means that many can take. Then they create distinct values and means of achievement, and thus, it becomes a community of its own. According to Robert Merton's Strain Theory (1938), those who have no or limited social opportunities and the means to attain the conventional goals come up with alternative means to attain those goals. Some could even substitute conventional goals that may be antisocial and illegal. This is seen as a reaction against status frustration (Cohen 1955).

Max Weber (1968) had treated social classes as status groups with special lifestyles, and Thornstein Veblen ([1899] 1957) and Herbert Gans (1975) had offered accounts of the relation between social classes and culture. Aesthetic taste, such as fashion, is not a matter of individual choice but is determined by one's class position. As early as 1961, Kurt Lang and Gladys Engel Lang questioned in their *Collective Dynamics* (1961) whether public taste is first manufactured and then disseminated through organized channels and foisted upon the mass, or whether changes in the moods and life conditions lead to irrational and widespread changes of taste even without promotion (1961: 466). Using Christian Dior's New Look of 1947 as an example, they explain that the collective change in taste which is an objective trend is dictated not by an organized fashion industry but by the capricious nature of fashion itself which is resisted and accepted by people (Lang and Lang 1961).

Pierre Bourdieu (1984) analyzed tastes in painting, books, food, and fashion, among others. For fashion, he put forward a theory regarding the aesthetic and functional components of dress. For the working class, dress does not serve more than a utilitarian function among them. It may have an aesthetic function, too, but it is a different kind of aesthetics, one that is often dismissed by the dominant class, according to Bourdieu.

The taste for sneakers, rap music, graffiti art, and other artistic preferences can also be analyzed within Bourdieu's theoretical framework of class and taste. Bourdieu showed for France what Herbert Gans (1975) had found in the United States. There are coherent social-class differences in the consumption of culture. Bourdieu argued that people's class positions and aspirations are closely connected to how they lead their lives and what they consume. Fundamental ways of living and social environments, which Bourdieu called *habitus*, are what determines one's taste preferences. It is often inherited materially from the previous generations and also through socialization. *Habitus* is not innate or inborn.

It has been repeatedly implied that whatever taste that is appreciated by the wealthy dominant class is the legitimate taste and considered as the right, sophisticated taste. During the First Wave Sneaker Phenomenon up until the mid-1980s when there were limited and scarce structural opportunities for the minority youngsters, they found opportunities in the sneaker subculture which allowed them to express their versions of aesthetics. An obsessive sneaker collection is not inherently deviant, but it is not something people in the dominant culture do or aspire to do since they are able to take conventional means to attain status and prestige. Members of the subculture are said to reject conformity, but they are constantly looking for another group where they can conform to and find alternative ways.

As early as 1970, John Irwin wrote: "American people are becoming aware of the subcultural variation in their society and are experiencing subcultural relativism" ([1970] 2005: 76). This trend has intensified even further in this day and age, especially in New York. There is a shift in people's ideas about values and norms. There are variations in aesthetic taste in different cultures and subcultures. There is no such a thing as one legitimate taste or dominant taste. It is not about taste being good/bad or sophisticated/unsophisticated, it is different in every "subcultural context."

The Second Wave post-Jordan Sneaker Phenomenon

The Second Wave starts with the release of a new sneaker brand called Nike Air Jordan 1 (often abbreviated as AJ1) in 1985, which was named after an NBA (National Basketball Association) basketball player, Michael Jordan. This shoe changed the sneaker phenomenon completely, brought the subculture from underground to upperground, and made the group of sneaker enthusiasts more visible, while the old-timer fans are disappointed with this large-scale diffusion because the gatekeeping function has now shifted from the collectors to the sneaker industry. Ben Osborne, editor of SLAM, the basketball magazine, writes (2013: 9): "The sneaker-collecting game of today has blown up beyond anything I ever imagined, and trust me when I say that even the most optimistic Jordan brand employees never expected all this either."

Osborne further explains that there are pros and cons for the worldwide sneaker popularity (Osborne 2013). The old-time collectors do not consider today's "sneakerheads" as real and authentic because the inauthentic ones spend all their disposable income on sneakers and post them on social media and go to sneaker conventions that take place in different cities in the United States or Europe. But at the same, as the sneaker popularity spread to the world, having a job that is related to sneakers, such as publishing a sneaker magazine, puts one in the center of the world. Whether one likes the current sneaker phenomenon or not, the market has changed drastically as we entered the Second Wave Sneaker Phenomenon and even the Third Wave.

Nike, basketball, and Michael Jordan

Not all sneaker enthusiasts are basketball fans, but those who choose to wear Nike Air Jordan sneakers are. They are Michael Jordan's signature sneakers. Jordan is a former American professional basketball player. He joined the NBA's Chicago Bulls in 1984 and later Washington Wizards. His prolific scoring made him a huge NBA star. Because of the height of his leap in the air, he earned a nickname "Air Jordan." He won the championship with the Chicago Bulls three years consecutively in 1991, 1992, and 1993. He then retired abruptly but came back and rejoined the Bulls in 1995. He once again led the team to the championship in 1996, 1997, and 1998. He retired the second time in 1999 and came back to NBA with the Wizards for two seasons from 2001 and 2003.[5]

Nike initially signed a five-year deal with Jordan for 2.5 million dollars, and they unexpectedly made about 1.3 million dollars in the first year. Jordan started wearing his own signature sneakers on the basketball court in 1984, which grabbed basketball fans' attention with a unique color combination. The first

AJ shoe in the black and red model was initially banned by the NBA because it was against the league's color rules, but he still wore them three times not conforming to the rule. His fans and sneaker collectors loved his sneakers even more because of the rebellious and the anti-conformist attitude of Jordan who did not obey the NBA rules. Nike took this opportunity and generated a hype by promoting "Banned by the NBA" commercials, and by paying his $5,000 fine at every game.

AJ1 is the only model that has a swoosh, the most recognizable Nike logo and also had the greatest number of colorways, twenty-three in total. It was sold with two sets of shoelaces to match the different colors. Because of its phenomenal commercial success, a series of AJ sneakers are produced every year in multiple colorways and designs for each model, and they give the collectors the reasons to purchase new pairs every season (Plates 2.3–2.5). An iconic mark of a Jumpman logo started with Air Jordan III in 1988.

It created mainstream consciousness on a global scale, and with the start of the AJ shoes, sneaker collection began to slowly receive the attention of the mass audience. As one of his fans said to me: "it was always exciting to see which pair Jordan was going to wear in his game. It was just as exciting as watching him play basketball."

Endorsement of famous athletes existed before Michael Jordan, but it had never been this successful. Jordan personified power, status, wealth, and everything that boys and young men strive to achieve during their life time. "To this day, no player's line comes close to Nike's Jordan-branded footwear, sales of which reached $2.5 billion last year. Over all, basketball sneaker sales made up $4.5 billion of the total $21 billion athletic shoes business, according to Princeton Retail Analysis" (Glickson 2014: A3).

The industry realized that the sneaker enthusiasts were also attracted to the older editions which some could not get, and they started making the "retro" models, which were the original ones with some minor changes in the design. It was easier, more efficient, and less risky than putting out brand new designs. The major sneaker companies became savvy in marketing their products and made a group of athletes into mega stars while suggesting a new kind of lifestyle with sneakers. Even NBA has become a brand along with their players.

The historical significance of red

Many of the sneakers endorsed by powerful and successful athletes and rap musicians have red in their designs with distinct names, such as Air Yeezy 2 "Red October," Nike Air Penny 5 "Red Eagle," Nike Kobe 8 "Red Camo," Nike LeBron 10 EXT "Red Suede" PE, Air Jordan IV "Red October," and Ewing 33 Hi "Red Suede," among many others.

The "red" color has had significant meanings in historical footwear studies. Red heels in seventeenth- and eighteenth-century European courts were also considered a symbol of nobility and status. While we associate contemporary red shoes or red soles with female footwear and rarely with male footwear, red shoes and red heels were favored by men of the upper class. For instance, bright red heels were favored by King Louis XIV of France and during his reign, red high heels, while already an established fashion, became a regulated expression of political privilege: only those granted access to the French court were permitted to wear them (Boucher 1987: 305; Semmelhack 2011: 225).

In her informative study on red shoes "Sex and Sin: The Magic of Red Shoes" (2011: 272–289), Hilary Davidson explains the social power imbued in red shoes:

> By combining two potent and ambiguous elements, red shoes assume complex symbolic power. Historically, red shoes conveyed authority, wealth and power, linked to the status-enhancing cost of red dyes such as madder, kernes, cochineal and lac. Red shoes were the prerogative first of Roman senators, and later solely for the emperor. Popes have worn red since the thirteenth century, while both Edward IV and Henry VIII were buried in red shoes as emblems of their monarchical power. In the seventeenth century, Louis XIV wore red heels on his shoes as a symbol of the divine right of the king....this style filtered down. Through imitation, to the aristocracy of both sexes and by the eighteenth century it had become a sign of aspirational fashionability. The cost and quality of shoes made of fine, red morocco leather meant that they were status symbols. (Davidson 2011: 274)

Then, Davidson discusses the literary allusions of the red shoes in Hans Christian Andersen's story of *The Red Shoes* written in 1845 and connects his use of the shoes within the context of sexuality, magic, and gender. It tells a story of "wildly passionate behavior and untrammeled female sexuality and mobility made possible by a pair of red shoes" (Davidson 2011: 288).[6]

The production of new sneaker technologies

There is no subculture where members are so much in pursuit of adopting something new which is one of the most important characteristics of "fashion" (see Chapter 4), and it is not only the consumers of sneakers but also the sneaker manufacturers that compete in developing the latest technology in the construction of sneakers. This is a subculture made of both the consumers and the producers that explicitly celebrate overt competition in attaining a status. They want the best and the latest sneakers with the most advanced technology. It is not just the design or the pattern of the shoe that is new, but also the technology embedded inside the shoe. As the subculture begins to surface on the upperground and the popularity begins to spread widely, the competition is accelerated and heated. The companies provide the reasons for them to compete and try to satiate the appetite of the enthusiasts so that they are constantly entertained and not bored by this "sneaker game." When we trace the invention and the development of the first sneakers and the sneaker companies, the emphasis had always been about the construction and the technological advancement of the shoes in order to achieve the maximum performance in sports.

The invention of vulcanization and sneakers

In his book *Sneakers* (1978), Walker gives a detailed chronology of the development of sneakers and explains that it was Wait Webster of New York who was granted a patent for his process of attaching rubber soles to boots and shoes in 1832 (Walker 1978: 15), but those shoes were still fragile and came apart easily. Then after multiple trials and experiments, Charles Goodyear managed to come up with something more solid, strong, and stable. He developed this process further and invented the vulcanization process which is the process of melting rubber and fabric together. According to Merriam-Webster.com, vulcanization is the process of treating crude or synthetic rubber or similar plastic material chemically to give it useful properties, such as elasticity, strength, and stability. Goodyear patented this process in 1844. This technological breakthrough is the result of the invention of rubber-soled shoes, and thus it revolutionized the sneaker industry forever. This mixture was molded to create a sole for shoes that had a tread design. Thus, Goodyear is known as the father of sneakers.

Similarly, in the United Kingdom, companies were eager to create better sneakers. In 1890, Joseph William Foster, the founder of the company Boulton in the UK (now known as Reebok) and also a runner, added spikes to the bottom of the plimsolls and invented the first running spikes. By 1905, he was selling them as "Foster's Running Pumps." He named his company J.W. Foster and Sons, and his grandsons took control over the business in 1958 and named it Reebok (Walker 1978: 15).

In 1916, Goodyear and US Rubber Company which was composed of thirty small companies, decided to manufacture shoes entirely with rubber soles called "Keds," and they were the first true sneakers and an early form of athletic shoes in 1917. Keds launched a line of sneakers called "Pro-Keds" targeted mainly at basketball players. This also later became the company name. They eventually became known as sneakers because of the rubber sole, and they could "sneak" around and "sneak" up on people silently.

Similarly, Converse developed their basketball shoes in 1917, initially known as the All Star and later renamed as the Converse All Star Chuck Taylor. They were also the sneakers made specially for basketball players. Charles H. Taylor, who was a former basketball player with the Akron Firestones, joined the Convers sales team. He traveled around the country promoting them to basketball players. By 1923, he started to get involved in the production and design process of the shoe. They became known as "Chucks." They were initially black, and then off-white ones were made, and a variety of new colors came out afterward. They remained extremely popular, and by 1968, Converse had dominated 80 percent of the sneaker industry (Heard 2003: 42). And Chuck Taylor was inducted into the basketball Hall of Fame. By 1997, 550 million pairs had been sold. Converse coined the term "limousines for the feet" to describe the added value of fame, prestige, and star status associated with their shoes through endorsement by professional basketball players (Gill 2011: 377).

Competition in sneaker technology since 1980s

Major sneaker companies continue to produce and enhance their sneaker technology. Before and after the launch of Air Jordans, Nike has produced a number of popular sneakers and is constantly developing and upgrading new technology embedded in the structure of the sneakers. As the competition among sneaker enthusiasts became intense, so did the technological development of the sneakers.

Nike has been a forerunner in the technology competition introducing sneakers with cutting-edge functions. As early as 1974, one of the founders of Nike and a former track and field coach, Bill Bowerman, poured rubber chemicals into his wife's waffle maker to create the sole of the sneaker, coming up with a waffle sneaker. Nike first incorporated the air system in 1979 in the Tailwind, the first shoe within the patented air-sole cushioning system. Then it was used in the Air Force 1 and Air Ace. There is the everlasting fascination with Nike Air Force 1 that came out in 1982 and discontinued for several years and was relaunched in 1986 (Plate 2.6). The name comes from the plane that is used to transport the president of the United States. Garcia explains his first impression on the shoes:

> I honestly thought they were hiking shoes upon first glance. I had never seen a bottom so thick for a baseball shoe. It was like a dream come true for someone like myself, who played outdoors so much…. The heel was unsurpassed for comfort, the leather was thick as shit but still supple so I had mobility, and the padding on the ankle was bushy. (Garcia 2003: 119)

It is a simple white pair of sneakers without any decoration, and this could be part of the broader concept of aesthetic minimalism, as Vainshtein points out

(2009: 94) that minimalism can be a sign of sartorial understatement manifesting the priority of functional construction and geometry of the basic form stripped of superfluous embellishment.

In 1987, Marion Frank Rudy, an inventor from California, suggested to put air in the sole for better performance and approached Nike with his idea, and the technology was used in Nike Air Max 1. It was the start of the technological development of the air system that used pressurized gas encapsulated in polyurethane in sneakers. The Nike Air Max was the first shoe that allowed one to see its technology inside the shoe (Plate 2.7). Then in 1995, Nike Air Max 95 was released. This time an air unit was visible at the front of the shoe, while Air Max 360 had air all around the shoe. Zoom Air which was released in 1995 had air which was lighter than Air Max, and the wearer felt much closer to the ground. In 1997, Air Foamposite came out as Penny Hardaway's signature sneakers, which has been relaunched in different colors and designs multiples times ever since (Plates 2.8–2.11).

In the twenty-first century, Nike became even more aggressive in the technology development. In 2000, Nike Air Woven was designed by Mike Avenie which looks like basket weave. This was first released in Tokyo prior to its launch in London and New York, and each country had a different color which meant that for a particular color one would need to fly to the country or ask someone in that country to send it to him. In 2004, a very light sneaker called Nike Free that felt like bare feet was launched. In 2008, Lunarlon Foam, known as Lunar, made out of springy and light material was developed with help from NASA (National Aeronautics and Space Administration). Hyperfuse, which was a combination of mesh and thin layers of plastic and was ultra light, was released in 2010. More recently, in 2012, Flyknit made out of light-weight and seamless knitted fabric was unveiled (Plate 2.12). Nike continues to push the technology boundaries, and that is what fascinates the sneaker enthusiasts because this game never ends.

While Nike is a leader in the current technology competition, Reebok developed Reebok Pump in 1989, which had a chamber with a built-in inflatable mechanism and also had air around the shoe, not under the shoe like Nike's air. The technology was advanced further and they launched Reebok Instapump in 1994 which was a success. It is a shoe without shoe laces and the goal was to customize fit with inflatable air. The first Instapump was designed in neon yellow, red, and black. They also changed the sole design from the conventional full-length sole to having a big dent in the middle of the sole unit. They also used stretchy material to gain a better fit. Sneakers without shoelaces was a creative idea as a wearer simply had to press the pumping unit rubber button to inflate the tongue to fit his foot. Puma developed a similar shoe called Puma Disc Blaze without shoelaces in 1992 (Plate 2.13). Asics Gel, launched by Asics, was a shoe that used soft gel-like compound within the shoe which absorbed impact while adidas had Boost Foam with cushioning system that revolutionized new foam.

While Vans's presence in the industry may not be as strong and prominent as Nike, Puma, or adidas, they have loyal followers and customers because of their specialized sneakers for skateboarders. Their soles were very thick, making them resistant to the ground friction. Steven Van Doren, son of Paul Van Doren, the founder, says (quoted in Palladini 2009: 14): "In order to make the shoes stand out, he [Paul Van Doren] made the soles as thick so they would wear longer. He also wanted to use pure crepe rubber with no filler like a lot of other shoe manufacturers used. That decision ended up changing our company when skateboarders discovered our now famous rubber sole." The popularity of Vans shoes had a major impact on other companies to produce similar shoes. Nike started a new line called the Nike SB (Skateboarding) Dunk with extra-padded tongue for durability, which is necessary for skateboarding sneakers. The major sneaker companies continue to compete, share, and provide new ideas about technology.

Controversies and debates to strengthen the subcultural bond

There is no shortage of sneakers that created commotion, heated debates, and controversies. The names and designs are offensive, insulting, and demeaning to some groups of people. But what is ironic is that when there are controversies about new sneakers, there are heated exchanges on Twitter and Instagram, and people unwittingly strengthen their bonds with fellow sneaker enthusiasts. Bengtson wrote an online article on "The 25 Most Controversial Things that Ever Happened in Sneakers"[7] and listed the sneakers that were controversial to the public as well to the sneaker enthusiasts.

In 2012, a new pair of sneakers designed by Jeremy Scott and adidas with ankle shackles created uproar on social media. It was scheduled to be released in August 2012, but adidas decided not to produce them. There were intense discussions online that this reminded a particular racial group of slavery. Reverend Jesse Jackson, an American civil rights activist and a Baptist minister, called the sneakers "slave shoes" and released the following comment:

> The attempt to commercialize and make popular more than 200 years of human degradation, where blacks were considered three-fifths human by our Constitution, is offensive, appalling and insensitive. (Reverend Jesse Jackson quoted in Considine 2012: E7)

Scott's explanation was that he got his inspirations from his own collection of soft toys, and he posted the pictures of the toys online, although he never publically apologized in person, but adidas canceled its release. Adidas had previously faced another controversy in 2006. A cartoon character of an Asian face on the tongue of the sneaker was criticized by the Asian American organizations as racist. This character was drawn by a cartoonist Barry Mcgee who is half-Chinese and half-Caucasian. He explained that the face is an image of himself when he was young. This was initially a limited edition with only a thousand pairs in production, but the ones that were still unsold were taken off the shelves.

Nike also has had similar share of controversies. In 1997, Nike produced Air Berkin with ketchup and mustard colors with a logo on the heel that resembled the Arabic spelling of "Allah" which created a huge commotion within the Muslim community. It was recalled, and Nike later replaced the design on the heel with the Nike logo. Similarly, the problem of Air Jordan XII Retro Rising Sun in 2009 was an insole design which was similar to a symbol of Japan's Imperialism, and that was offensive to Koreans and Chinese, who at the time were Japan's enemies. Nike decided to replace the insole with a simple design. In 2012, Nike SB Dunk Low "Black & Tan" was released in commemoration for the St. Patrick's Day and named after Ireland Beer that is made from Guinness and Herb named Black & Tan, but it is also the name of a group that was hired by the British government to suppress the Irish by force, so this name was offensive to the Irish people, but Nike decided to continue with the release.

Furthermore, Converse released a pair called Loaded Weapon in 2003. This was a retro version of the pair worn by NBA basketball stars, Larry Byrd and Magic Jackson, called "Weapon" in 1985. But, in 2003, some NBA players were arrested for possession of illegal weapons, so there were concerns about whether the name would encourage gun violence among sneaker enthusiasts. The company explained that Loaded implies the name of the cushion on the bottom and weapon refers to the original model of this pair of sneakers and continued to release the shoes.

Whether these controversial designs are created intentionally or unintentionally is unknown, but they surely create a tumult within the community as communication in the Third Wave Sneaker Phenomenon is extremely rapid. Ironically, problems, issues, crisis, and controversies bind people together (Durkheim 1897) because we, as a collective group, make an attempt to solve that problem and overcome a crisis, and thus looking at the same direction with a common goal to achieve. With today's use of social media, the sneaker enthusiasts discuss, debate, and argue on Twitter and Instagram, and that further strengthens and reinforces the bond among those who are passionate about sneakers.

Conclusion

A community of sneaker enthusiasts in the 1970s enjoyed their underground status creating their own aesthetic values and norms about sneakers and kept themselves hidden from the mainstream. But with the arrival of a new series of sneakers, the process and the structural mechanism of sneaker collection has transformed. It still remains to be a subculture that binds the members with sneakers, but it has emerged on the upper surface from underground. Sneaker chase and hunting have become a game in which boys and young men compete to acquire exclusive sneakers because that is a way to earn their peer's respect. At the same time, sneaker companies make sure that they continue to provide new models so that the game of sneaker hunting continues. The gatekeepers for the sneaker subculture used to be the collectors themselves, but as the industry began to realize that there is a market for the youths who are thirsty for cool and fashionable sneakers, the industry began to take charge, and they contribute to sustaining the subculture of sneakers.

3

SNEAKERS AS A SYMBOL OF MANHOOD: WEARING MASCULINITY ON THEIR FEET

As indicated in Chapter 1, footwear represents social and cultural meanings, and in addition, footwear has historically been a strong marker of gender, and it clearly indicates whether it is a male shoe or a female shoe. Clothing also marks gender differences in our modern democratic society, but the boundary between the two is often believed to be blurring, and some fashion designers, such as Rad Hourani and Telfar Clemens, do not wish to categorize their collections as menswear or womenswear, claiming that clothing can and should be unisex and androgynous. But historical and contemporary footwear distinguishes men from women. Women wear heels, sandals, and flip flops, while men wear lace-up leather shoes and sneakers. We attach different images to different types of shoes. We hear very little about unisex footwear that is interchangeably worn between the two sexes. Shoes are where gendered identities are most saliently expressed. There were also functional differences between the two types of footwear.

Chapter 3 looks at the gender component of footwear and the sneaker subculture since contemporary footwear is a gendered item that draws a line between male and female and the social implications behind these two. When contemporary footwear is discussed, it is often female footwear and female feet that are the main topic. As a gendered object, many have paid attention to women's high heels that are not very functional but beautiful, often with erotic implications. On the other hand, sneakers are male footwear that is hardly ever treated as a fetish object and seems to have only the utilitarian element, and it is assumed there is not much to discuss. However, as high heels are the ultimate symbol of femininity, limited edition sneakers represent masculinity. The shoe is a complex and primary marker of gender difference, a complex messenger that can trick, bewilder, or allure (Steele 2011: 270). While Steele was mostly talking about female footwear, such as stiletto heels and boots, this is applicable to sneakers as well.

Like many other subcultures in the West, the sneaker subculture has been primarily occupied by boys and young men. Girls and women play a secondary role. Most of the sneakers are made and sold for men, and there are fewer choices in design and size for women. While the pursuit of adornment and self-display has been a female terrain, sneakers that are associated with sports and the incessant use of technology by the enthusiasts make it a male affair.

No other subculture other than the sneaker subculture is bounded by one object of dress. Female high-heel enthusiasts do not form a subculture in the same way the sneaker subculture does. While a group of punks is identified by ripped pants and safety pins, or bikers with leather jackets, the items of dress are not the reasons why they belong to the group. Subcultural theorists explain that youth subcultures in general are a working-class male phenomenon, but I argue that members of the sneaker subculture today are not necessarily from the working class as it once was during the First Wave Sneaker Phenomenon. But it is definitely a male fashion phenomenon. One of the most important social variables that continues to be reinforced is "gender." Sneakers as an object are used to manifest their strong sense of masculinity, although these two, masculinity and fashion, are opposing concepts (see Chapter 4).

Muggleton and Weinzierl point out that "intellectual hegemony" of the Gramscian-semiotic approach of the CCCS appear to be in the advanced stage of dissolution (2003: 5), but I argue that the hegemonic idea of masculinity is strongly in tact in the sneaker subculture. Through my fieldwork and face-to-face interaction and communication with the sneaker fans, I investigate sociologically why and how the maleness of the sneaker subculture is established and perpetuated and study the process through which men construct their masculinity, such as the practice of sneaker collection and trading, the pursuit of the latest and the most limited edition sneakers using social capital, and the latest technology. In this way, we can revisit the idea of sex and gender in relation to the sneaker subculture as part of fashion and dress studies.

Footwear and gender

There is a consensus among dress and fashion scholars that human footwear was not always gendered, but there are different accounts as to when footwear became gender-specific. The distinction between ladies' shoemakers and men's shoemakers in the eighteenth century clearly indicates that footwear was gendered.

The production of men's and women's shoes implied diverse skills as the products themselves were essentially dissimilar. While men's shoes were normally made of leather, women's shoes had silk, satin, cloth, or brocade uppers. In the same way, boots, masculine wear only until the 1900s, presented similar gender differences. (Riello 2006: 35)

Similarly, Sue Blundell (2011) writes that the gender differences between male and female of footwear were present even in Ancient Greece, and Xenophon (430–354 BC), a Greek historian and philosopher, tells that there were shoemakers who specialized in the manufacturing of either male or female footwear. A type of footwear was a strong indicator of one's gender rather than one's wealth and status (Blundell 2011: 35). Walford explains the relationship between clothing and footwear and that the shoes became a clear marker of gender after the fourteenth century:

Footwear and clothing were similar for both sexes until the fourteenth century. Shoes were generally flat-soled with almond-shaped toes. Pointed toes appeared in the eleventh century but rarely in an exaggerated form.... But in the mid-fourteenth century, however, men's clothing tightened and shortened, bringing shoes into full view and making them prime candidates for elaboration. The toes of men's shoes became so long that they protruded several inches in front of the shoe and were known as "crakowes" in England or "poulaines" in France, after their supposed Polish origin. (Walford 2007: 11)

Various accounts and scholarly studies on *poulaines* indicate that it was clearly a male footwear.

Both western and non-western societies culturally emphasize the distinctions between the two sexes resulting in the pronounced sex differences by putting women in skirts and high heels and men in pants and sneakers. In this way, we make categorical differences. Irvin Goffman's seminal text on *Gender Advertisements* (1979) offers a social constructionist approach to gender differentiations based on 500 advertisements and news photographs. He talks about interactionist manifestations of gender differences which he calls "gender display." Biological differences should not be the explanations for the social or cultural differences as gender scholars all agree. According to Goffman (1979: 8), "there is only a schedule for the portrayal of gender...only evidence of the practice between the sexes of choreographing behaviourally a portrait of relationship." Society forces, motivates, and encourages people to play their gender script, including how to dress as a male and a female, through which they create their respective gender identity. And their identities are marked through dress and footwear. Supposedly, gender, which represents sex, is something that should not be confusing to the public.

Similarly, Michael Kimmel, an expert in gender studies, claims that gender is often limited to women's experiences and perspectives, but we need to include both masculine and feminine perspectives (2012), and we as a society focus on the differences rather than similarities between the sexes while there are more commonalities than differences. Those differences are often accentuated by clothing and footwear. He illustrates that gender is not merely an element of individual identity, but a socially constructed institutional phenomenon that is reproduced over time. Men and women are playing a role of gender dress performance.

High heels: Mobility for men and immobility for women

Much of the literature on contemporary footwear is about women's shoes, high heels in particular, but historical evidence shows us that high heels were initially worn by both men and women. According to Swann (1982: 7), who traces the history of shoes in Europe, heels were introduced in the late sixteenth century which probably developed from Venetian type *chopine*. Heeled footwear began in Western Europe, and different shoes designs from the Persians, Ottomans, Crimean Tartars, Polish and Ukrainian Cossack, and Indian Mughals could have been possible sources for the high heels. While scholars have been debating the exact origin of heels, many scholars, including Elizabeth Semmelhack (2011: 225) and Philip Perrot (1996: 70–73), explained that high heels had become a symbol of wealth, style, and status and were worn by men, women, and children of the upper classes by the early to middle part of the seventeenth century. In contrast, low heels with rounded toes made out of strong leather uppers were signs of inferior social status (Riello 2006: 63).

However, men's high heels had practical functions. McDowell explains the functional purpose of men's high heels:

> Horse-riding, for pleasure or transport, has been an overwhelmingly masculine prerogative and this fact has had a considerable effect on the design of heels for men's shoes. High heels for men helped keep the foot in the stirrup and aided control of the horse during hard riding. They could not be functional if the heel was too narrow and tapering, as it would be liable to snap; and if it were too high, walking difficult. So male high heels were a response to a practical need; they had to be dual-purpose, suitable for riding and convenient for walking. (McDowell 1989: 11)

In addition, McNeil and Riello (2011c: 95) revisit the idea of gender and class in relation to footwear as many believe that both men and women wore equally high and beautiful shoes until the Industrial Revolution, but they argue that it is a misconception. They explain the environmental conditions of the dirty streets with rubbish during the first half of the eighteenth century, which led to the gender differences in the shoes. Riello explains:

Gender differences did not simply imply functional differences in the construction, form, and materials of footwear, but were often the subject of negotiation and representation thorough the medium of footwear (Riello 2006: 87).

At the beginning of the nineteenth century women found themselves increasingly confined to private spaces. The public street and the outdoor space became places of masculine prerogative. Women as "angels of the house" were further constrained in their mobility by the use of small silk shoes. This "domestication" of femininity coincides with the cultural rise of a separate sphere, in which women were increasing excluded from public life. (Riello 2006: 89)

Thus, male footwear always had practical functions even in high heels making them mobile. In contrast, female footwear made women immobile. It shows that no footwear is more masculine than sneakers if functionality and mobility are the primary characteristics of male footwear.

The gender difference in footwear marked male power. Social differences in terms of power and prestige were represented through footwear. As Trasko explains:

Over the centuries shoes have also expressed social power, symbolizing men's authority over women and effectively enslaving women by circumscribing heir mobility. The symbolism can clearly be seen in some of the rituals of the marriage ceremony. In the Middle Ages, for example, a father' authority over his daughter was passed to her husband by means of her shoe, In other instances the groom might hand the bride a shoe; to put it on was to concede that she had become his subject. (Trasko 1989: 12)

Women's dress, including heels, a long skirt, and long hair, makes them immobile and less functional because that was what meant to be "feminine and elegant" in a patriarchal society. As early as the late nineteenth century, Veblen remarked:

The more elegant styles of feminine bonnets go even farther towards making work impossible than does the man's high hat. The woman's shoe adds the so-called French heel to the evidence of enforced leisure afforded by its polish; because the high heel obviously makes any, even in a higher degree of the skirt and the rest of the drapery which characterises woman's dress. The substantial reason for our tenacious attachment to the skirt is just this: it is expensive and it hampers the wearer at every turn and incapacitates her for all useful exertion. The like is true of the feminine custom of wearing the hair excessively long. (Veblen [1899]1957: 171)

A male material object that binds subcultural members

Many subcultural theorists, especially those who draw from the CCCS traditions, discuss a specific subculture in regard to the group's outward look and style. Hebdige conducted a semiotic analysis of the punk subculture and talked about how the items that the members adopted had meanings that were different from the conventional ones:

> A pin, a plastic clothes peg, a television component, a razor blade, a tampon—could be brought within the province of punk (un)fashion. Anything within or without reason could be turned into part of what Vivien Westwood called "confrontation dressing" so long as the rupture between "natural" and constructed context was clearly visible.... Objects borrowed from the most sordid of contexts found a place in the punks' ensembles: lavatory chains were draped in graceful arcs across chests encased in plastic bin-liners. Safety pinks were taken out of their domestic "utility" context and worn as gruesome ornaments through the check, ear or lip. (Hebdige 1979: 107)

Similarly, in his "Rethinking the Subcultural Commodity: The Case of Heavy Metal T-shirt Culture(s)" (2007: 64), Andy Brown examined the commodification of a heavy-metal T-shirt that had the significant meanings to the youth culture that surrounds metal music, and the strong consumer demand for commercially produced metal-style T-shirts which is used in the formation of youth cultural identities and experiences. This item of clothing allows metal youth groups to make distinctions between themselves and others like many other clothing found in various subcultures as their informal dress code. Brown writes (2007: 72): "Its t-shirts were seen as heavily 'masculinist' and 'exclusionary' in a way that other t-shirts were not." However, in both of these case studies in Hebdige's and Brown's research, clothing or their styles are the means to express their subcultural ideology and values. They are not united by the object or the style to begin with; dress plays a secondary role in bringing the members together.

For sneaker enthusiasts, the sneakers are the very reason why they mobilize, socialize, and communicate. Their values, beliefs, norms, and attitudes are centered around sneakers. During the First Wave, sneakers were part of hip-hop culture, and the way they dressed was an expression of anti-mainstream sentiments, frustrations, anger, or hatred. But once they went above the surface, their social message began to transform. Sneakers became the object of desire to be on the winner's side and not a symbol of resistance, and they are like those who wear metal-style T-shirt because it looks "cool" (Brown 2007).

Once subcultures are commodified, subcultural objects can be transformed into "fashion." Those who value the sense of marginality would deplore such circumstances as they wish to remain underground at all times. No matter how widely the sneaker popularity spreads transcending boundaries, one latent hidden message behind the subculture is that they strongly maintain the gender division, and that they are in full control.

The exploration of masculinity in subcultures

Large macro-scale social structures in relations to sex, gender, and sexuality issues are constituted by personal practices on a micro level of one's personal life (Mills 1959). In social sciences, sex and gender are analyzed as separate entities and concepts, although people use them interchangeably as if they mean the same. As R. W. Connel writes:

> For many people it is threatening even to see these patterns as social. It is comforting to think the patterns are "natural" and that one's own femininity or masculinity is therefore proof against challenge. Western intellectuals, by and large, have helped this evasion. Thomism through Marxism to functionalism and systems theory, have taken the gender arrangements of the day pretty much for granted. (Connel 1987: 17)

As Connell suggested, masculinity is not a natural outcome of those with male organs and physical traits but is a socially constructed idea and practice. A complex system of socialization process in terms of "gender construction" begins and makes sure that appropriate gender identities and behaviors are learnt. We learn our social and cultural rules that make a society and social order possible. There is no inherent connection between sex, which is biology, and gender, which is cultural and social; gender is an expression of sex. The two are not naturally or innately correlated.

Contemporary studies on gender prove to us repeatedly that a gender hierarchy and stereotypical and hegemonic ideas about men and women are artificially produced and reproduced. At the same time, there are efforts to get rid of the gender barriers which also means there could be reverse attempts to maintain them, and the sneaker subculture is one of these communities that reinforces the traditional male qualities and excludes women.

Subcultures not only exclude women but also devalue them as unimportant and unnecessary in establishing their group. Hebdige explains (1988: 27) that girls have been relegated to a position of secondary interest within both sociological accounts of subculture and photographic studies of urban youth, and the masculinist bias is evident in the subcultures themselves. Girls and young women tend to be forgotten from the main picture of the subculture with a few exceptions, such as Riot Grrrls and Japanese Lolita girls.[1] McRobbie and Garber (1991: 4) also say that the objective and popular image of a subculture is like to be one that emphasizes male membership, male focal concerns, and masculine values.

The concept of subculture and the work of the early subcultural theorists have been largely criticized for focusing almost exclusively on working-class young men and as uncritically accepting particular definitions of crime and delinquency. But according to Brake (1980: 2), this is not surprising because an examination of the studies reveals not only a sexist perspective but also that the subcultures traditionally have been a place to examine centrally variations on several themes concerning masculinity.

On the whole, youth cultures and subcultures tend to be some form of exploration of masculinity. These are therefore masculinist, and I have tried to consider their effect on girls, and one distinct sign of the emancipation of young girls from the cult of romance, and marriage as their true vocation, will be the development of subcultures exploring a new form of femininity. (Brake 1980: vii)

As a young person trying to search for one's identity, gender is the closest and the easiest to grasp when they find it difficult to belong to and fit into other social groups. Members of the sneaker subculture manifest their masculine identity and manhood through their sneakers. They are literally wearing masculinity on their feet and at the same time reinforcing and reproducing the hegemonic idea about male and masculinity.

A focus on sneaker collectors and fans allows us to look at the social process of creating and playing the role of a male.

It is a way to prove that they are the true male members, and this is the case even for seemingly gender-neutral subcultures with a large group of female participants such as goth (Brill 2007). Women's social statuses in the subcultures are often on the periphery as the male member's girlfriend or partner. As one of the female sneaker enthusiasts said to me:

Women sneakerheads are never taken seriously. Guys think our boyfriend is a sneakerhead. They think I like sneakers just because my boyfriend likes sneakers. Or they think you just want guys' attention so you wear sneakers all the time. Sneakers for girls are so girly. You can't find masculine looking sneakers in women's sizes. Sneaker companies just don't make them. Female sneakerheads definitely have an inferior status.

Gender is analogous to class in that its structure creates inequalities and hierarchy. In order to maintain their maleness or masculinity, they need to segregate themselves from and exclude anything that has female or feminine qualities. Sneaker subculture as a community serves that function. As Brill writes:

> Given that subcultures have often been regarded as a vehicle through which young people resists dominant norms and structures, one might expect that such groups would have raised significant challenges to the boundaries of gender. However, there exists a long-standing connection between subcultures and dominant ideologies of masculinity. Girls have traditionally occupied a marginal position in the terrain of youth culture and academic studies about it. (Brill 2007: 111)

Youth subcultures resist the mainstream hegemonic values, but as far as gender is concerned, they not only maintain it but reinforce it. We live in a modern age where people are very much aware that any gender inequalities and sexism must be prevented, so we at least try to make men and women socially equal, and women are inclusive in every sphere of professional or leisure activities. But this belief does not exist among sneaker enthusiasts.

Male socialization through sneaker trading using social capital

Ever since Margaret Mead's groundbreaking study on sex and gender (1935),[2] many social scientific studies have shown that men and women are socialized differently in almost all known societies. According to Kahn-Harris, men in western societies strive to achieve qualities such as winning, emotional control, risk-taking, violence, dominance, self-reliance, power over women, disdain for homosexuals, and the pursuit of social status, all which are considered as mainstream masculine traits (2007: 143). Men are bonded through sharing activities, while women are bonded by sharing their feelings and emotions. Sneakers carry all the instrumental traits which are used to define male qualities. Gender-specific stereotypical behaviors, attitudes, beliefs, values, and norms are produced by various socializing agents, such as parents, relatives, schools, peers, and mass media. Sneaker enthusiasts and collectors reproduce the idea of male exclusivity that is symbolized by limited edition sneakers. Women do not stand in the rain or snow to get an exclusive pair of shoes, and that is a male activity. Men's actions and behavior are the reflection of who they are. Any female participation would jeopardize and tarnish their pure and authentic "maleness."

A sense of belonging through common subcultural knowledge

People strive to be included in a group, community, culture, or society to feel that they are accepted or welcomed. Human beings define themselves through group associations, whether it is a family, company, or school. A subculture is a community, organization, or group within the larger world of the dominant culture. They consist of individuals whose experiences have led them to have distinct worldviews. Members of a subculture challenge and question the mainstream ideas about social hierarchy, status, and authority. To experience a sense of belonging is a basic human need (Durkheim 1897) that is shared by subcultural members, including sneaker enthusiasts. A certain degree of social integration, such as attachment and regulations, influences a person's level of well-being. Membership in groups, especially peer groups, is a primary way that people meet this need. But even those who choose to deviate from the norm, they as a result conform to that deviant group to which they belong. We all belong somewhere. From your peer's perspective, you are an insider and not a deviant individual. Just like participants in other subcultures, sneaker enthusiasts are bonded by their "subcultural knowledge" that they can share only with their fellow enthusiasts. One of the sneaker enthusiasts tells me:

> I walk into an elevator, I see a guy inside. I look down at his sneakers, and I can tell if he is a sneakerhead or not. Then he looks at my feet, too. He can tell I'm a sneakerhead as well. We don't say anything. We just look at each other and each other's shoes, but both of us are quiet. There is silent communication. But we know, we belong to the same world. We are bonded immediately, and that's a great feeling.

They look at a pair of sneakers, and if that is an exclusive pair, they are able to tell its name, how it is made, who it was designed by, and how many pairs were released in which city, state, or country. Sharing the knowledge is a way to bond with other sneaker collectors, and it is always a way to earn a status within the community. One of the sneaker collectors said:

> Having hundreds of pairs doesn't mean anything. You have piles of sneakers in your room, but you don't know what exactly you have, you are not a real sneakerhead. A true sneakerhead knows the history behind the shoe. It doesn't mean anything if you are wearing the shoe that you know nothing about.

Knowledge is part of one's cultural capital (Bourdieu 1984), and subcultural knowledge is part of one's subcultural capital (Thornton 1995). As one of the sneaker collectors writes that a sneaker fan should be able to distinguish a reissue and an original (Serch quoted in Garcia 2003: 228): "Thou shalt not claim you know the difference between a reissue and an original when you don't, and thou shalt not claim original when it's a reissue. Thou shalt not claim old school sneakers when you are under twenty. It's a violation of code." Having the same knowledge is an indication that both of them are authentic insiders.

Furthermore, at the start of my empirical research in New York when I still was not aware of different names and types of sneakers, I asked a boy "what is the name of your sneaker?," he first looked puzzled wondering why I was asking him the question. Then he answered me slowly and clearly: "This is called *na-i-kee*." He must have assumed that I could not even recognize a famous Nike swoosh on his sneakers. But as time passed, my fieldwork progressed and I began to recognize the names of the sneakers and pointed out more specifically to their sneakers, "That's Nike Spiderman" (Plate 3.1), or "That's adidas × Jeremy Scott" (Plate 3.2). Their faces would light up and I could initiate a smooth conversation with them. I could feel firsthand that I was ever slightly accepted by them. At least they thought I knew what I was talking about.

The idea of subcultural capital suggested by Sarah Thornton (1995) includes the objects, practices, and beliefs that subcultural members use to distinguish themselves from outsiders and to prove their authentic status to insiders. Thornton builds upon the work of Bourdieu (1984), who discusses several types of capital, including cultural capital used to distinguish oneself from others and project a certain image. Thornton writes (1995: 11–12): "Subculturalists may use different less 'mainstream' objects to symbolize status, but they do so nonetheless .... they strive to be (and to be seen to be) 'in the know,' listening to the coolest underground music, wearing the right clothes, sporting the latest hairstyle, and knowing the moves to the latest dances."

It is not simply about wearing sneakers, but the process of buying a pair is also part of their informal membership criteria which is not found in other subcultural groups. For example, for a member of the punk group, it is not subculturally important for others to know the process of getting the jeans he is wearing. How you wear it or how to put together a punk style is more important and significant for the members. However, for the sneaker collectors, the actual buying process is part of the subcultural activity that they share. The strategies of finding the shoes, from whom, or which retailer does matter. Angela McRobbie writes in her "Second-Hand Dresses and the Role of the Ragmarket":

The act of buying and the process of looking and choosing still remain relatively unexamined in the field of cultural analysis. One reasons for this that shopping has been considered a feminine activity. Youth sociologists have looked mainly at the activities of adolescent boys and young men and their attention has been directed to those areas of experience which have a strongly masculine image. Leisure sphere which involve the wearing and displaying of clothes have been thoroughly documented, yet the hours spent seeking them out on Saturday afternoons continue to be overlooked. (McRobbie [1989] 2005: 132–133)

For sneaker enthusiasts, buying and selling sneakers is not a female activity. It not only requires subcultural knowledge but also subcultural social capital which is about whom you know and the connections you have, and that has always been important in the sneaker subculture before or after the Second Wave Sneaker Phenomenon. Bengtson explains how collectors used to look for cool sneakers:

Sneaker collecting started while Michael Jordan was still a North Carolina high schooler wearing adidas. People like Bobbio Garcia, Dante Ross and Michale Berrin were scouting whatever sneaker stores there were in the five boroughs of NYC (and beyond) for rare gems they could show off. (Bengtson 2013: 87)

No one knew or cared how many pairs were actually manufactured as long as it was a pair that no one else was wearing yet, and it looked "cool." But they needed the social capital to find these rare pairs. As one of the long-time collectors tells me: "Sneaker collection has lost its appeal completely with the invention of the Internet and the social media." Bengtson also adds:

And in those days before retro, there was only one way to get older models: You went digging. The process was simple enough: Find an old sporting goods store, befriend the owner, convince him or her to let you get into the darkest, dustiest corners of the back or basement, and get to searching. Before eBay, no one really knew what they had. And what did they have, really? The term "deadstock" initially meant just that—dead stock. The surplus inventory wasn't doing the store owners any good, and in many cases they were happy to get their shelf space back. Future classics were just there for the taking, often at pennies on the dollar. And instantly entire collections were born. (Bengtson 2013: 89)

Even after the Second Wave Sneaker Phenomenon, one's social capital weighed heavily in acquiring the pair he wanted. One of the collectors explains how not knowing a salesperson at a sneaker store meant:

When I was still in highschool, I went into a sneaker store and asked if they have a particular type of sneaker that just came out, and the guy said "no, it's all sold out." So I said, "Okay. Then, what about..." And before I even finished my sentence, he said "no we don't carry that either." I thought, what? Wait a minute, I haven't even said which brand or model, and he tells me he doesn't have it? But then I realized that I am just not welcome to this store. The store would not sell me anything.

People who work at sneaker stores are mostly sneaker collectors, and it is an envious job because they have access to the latest sneakers and possibly resell them to their friends or on the auction sites to get extra profits. This amounts to the collectors' social capital which becomes even more important and meaningful in an age where specific information or knowledge can be picked up and spread worldwide in a matter of seconds. Having an exclusive piece of information becomes even more valuable. Another sneaker collector, who is now an owner of the sneaker store in Brooklyn, said to me:

When the information spreads that there is going to be a limited edition, I call up stores, friends who work at sneaker stores and the company that is releasing this edition, and every where else that I can think of, and try to get that pair. It's all about connections that you have in this community. It's all about who you know and how well you know them.

The ability to use technology and social media is obviously a requirement to be a real "sneakerhead" to collect all the sneaker-related news, but in addition, one needs more than that to be a respected "sneakerhead" in the Third Wave Sneaker Phenomenon.

Distinguishing oneself from a female shopper as a male entrepreneur

Sneaker enthusiasts after the Second Wave have an official space, physical and virtual, to buy and sell their sneakers; they trade on the popular auction sites, such as ebay, or attend the sneaker conventions taking place in the United States carrying their sneakers, and at the same time, they learn "the art of trading up, sometimes earning a profit in the process" (Glickson 2014: A1). Many of them are technologically savvy. The use of technology and electronics is believed to be a male practice (Colatrella 2011; Lerman and Oldenziel 2003). Men enjoy the sense of control they get from handling technology-related gadgets and equipment. In addition, men like speed; competition is an activity-oriented trait attached mostly to men. While high-heel companies never advertise their production process or how their manufacturing was altered, sneaker companies actively promote and advertise their improved technology and the enhanced production processes embedded in sneakers. For women's shoes, they are all about how beautiful they look, and possibly some descriptions about comfort. But for sneakers, the outward appearance is not enough to convince male sneakers to purchase a new pair. Sneakers are judged by the internal characteristics as well, just as men are often judged by their intelligence, competency, and wealth.

The competition, communication, and interaction are shifting from a virtual space to a physical space. With an increasing popularity of sneakers and the expansion of sneaker enthusiasts and collectors, there are sneaker-related events happening around the world. Sneaker Convention (known as SneakerCon) was started in March, 2009, in New York, by three young men, two brothers Alan and Paris Vinogradoff and Yuming Wu. For the first event, only twenty companies took part to sell or resell sneakers, and anyone could attend with a $10 admission. Those who trade sneakers are not just professional vendors but also individuals who wish to trade their personal possessions. The event has now expanded to different cities in the United States, such as Cleveland, Fort Lauderdale, Houston, Washington DC, and Miami. Most recently, in December 2015, it took place at Jacob K. Javits Convention Center in New York with 10,000 participants (Plates 3.3–3.5).

One of the sneaker fans, a college student, carrying five pairs in boxes in a huge plastic bag that I met on the way to the convention in the pouring rain said to me:

> If I bought a pair for $100, I want to sell it at the same price or more and make some profit from it. I would never sell it for below $100. Then I would be losing my money. Not worth it. I've only worn these pair once or twice. I don't want to make them dirty because I know I would sell them in the future.

Young sneaker enthusiasts are becoming shrewd entrepreneurs learning how to negotiate and haggle in sneaker trading. Some would display their sneakers on the floor with price tags while others would walk around holding up a pair above their head and screaming out loud how much they want to sell it for and what size they have available. The sneaker conventions are providing the youths the space to conduct business and learn the trade at a young age. A young vendor turned away $98,000 in cash for his Nike Air Yeezy 2 "Red October" sneakers, designed by Kanye West and signed by the artist himself onstage at the Nassau Coliseum in February (Glickson 2014: A3). This is not female shopping. This is male entrepreneurship where serious business negotiations take place.

Another popular sneaker event, H-Town Sneaker Summit was established in December, 2003. It takes place twice a year in winter and summer in Houston, Texas. Sneaker enthusiasts look for rare items and also trade their sneakers with their peers. Similar events take place in Australia and Europe. Sneaker Pimps, a touring sneaker show, started in Sydney, Australia, in 2002, and celebrated its tenth anniversary in 2012 and toured throughout the United States. The event features rare, limited edition, vintage, sneakers, and one of the biggest attractions of Sneaker Pimps is the live painting and sneaker customizing that takes place at each show. Sneaker Pimps has visited more than sixty-two cities in countries, including Australia, New Zealand, the United States, Japan, Singapore, Taiwan, Korea, China, Thailand, Canada, Belgium, and the Philippines, making the world's largest sneaker and street art exhibition (Intercity 2008: 192). In 2015, they are traveling to India, Japan, Brazil, and Argentina among many other cities. In addition, the one in Europe is called Sneakerness, which takes place around Europe and is also expanding every year. It first started in Berlin 2008, then went to Vienne and Zurich in 2009, and finally went to Cologne, Zurich, and Vienna in 2010. In 2015, the event will take place in Zurich, Paris, Amsterdam, Warsaw, and Cologne.

In order to purchase new sneakers, the younger generation sneaker fans with limited budget and pocket money either sell their possessions or borrow money from their family and friends. Chase Reed was one of them who wanted to borrow $50 from his father, Troy Reed, who held onto the son's sneakers until he got the money back from his son. This was where the idea came from, and they opened the world's first Sneaker Pawn Shop in Harlem, New York, in 2014. They see firsthand how attached sneaker enthusiasts are to their possessions. Troy says:

Ninety-eight percent of our customers come back, pay back the money and take back their sneakers. For them, sneakers are not just footwear. It means more to them. There is a lot of emotional attachment to sneakers. Once, a kid left a worn out sneakers. It was pretty bad, and we didn't think he would come back. But he did. He paid back the money and took his sneakers back.

Objects begin to have a life of their own. Sneakers share the owner's emotions, sentiments, and experiences, and parting from them would be just as difficult as parting from your loved ones. The father-and-son team want to make their shop into a community space where sneaker enthusiasts can get together.

The culture of endorsement: The personification of success

Many sneaker enthusiasts agree that ever since the arrival of Michael Jordan in the basketball scene, it raised the awareness and popularity of sneakers to a new level. Jordan became a role model to many boys and young men who needed someone to look up to. Jordan was strong, powerful, rich, and charismatic. He possessed all the qualities that anyone would aspire to attain. He personified masculinity and success. They also vicariously enjoyed their status by wearing the sneakers endorsed by Jordan and many other popular athletes. In 1995, Michael Jordan, Grant Hill, and Shaquille O'Neal were each making more in shoe revenue than all NBA players combined had received for shoe deals during any year in the 1970s and possibly the entire decade (Vanderbilt 1998: 43). Osborne reminisces his passion for Jordan sneakers since his younger days:

> While in grammar school in suburban Westchester County, I rocked fat laces in the fourth grade. Fifth grade saw me fall in love with the Air Jordan I, as I wore, and wore out, three straight pairs over fifteen months. Sixth grade coincided with my getting Converse Weapons, because for a time it seemed that every star in the NBA besides MJ was wearing them. Middle school brought me the chance to start a little (caddying in basketball shoes? Sure, why not?) and making my own money. The local baseball-card store got some of it; basketball-shoe retailers got the rest. While still enamored with MJ and his growing line (I had all those 1s, never got the $100 IIs, then had multiples of the IIIs, IVs, and Vs), I also noticed how popular all of them were getting. And I wanted to be different. (Osborne 2013: 10)

The successful athletes, such as LeBron James, Patrick Ewing, and Kobe Bryant, are the key figures in producing "cool" and "fashionable" sneakers (Plates 3.6–3.9). Their participation and involvement in this sneaker game determine the sneaker collector's status and reputation. Just as fashion designers are the stars in the production of fashion, athletes are very much responsible in creating exclusive sneakers that symbolize their accomplishment and achievement. They personify success through their sneakers. Sports offer a clear black and white outcome: you are either a winner or a loser. The sneaker game may not be as clear as the sports, but they are very conscious of which ones signify status. Each sneaker company has endorsed famous athletes and came up with their signature sneakers. Wearing the right pair of sneakers grants some of the boys a feeling of confidence, a higher self-esteem, or a positive self-image since the sneakers personify success. They are hunting for sneakers, but at the same time, they are chasing the ideal image of a socially successful and a physically powerful male.

Sneaker language with an assertion of masculinity

Names and words are imbued with images, implications, and stereotypes. There is the particular rhetorical language found in the sneaker nicknames. Richard Buchanan in his article "Rhetoric, Humanism and Design" (1995) explains that products convey notions of value, meaning and style, and foster fantasy, intimacy, and desire with their potential consumers. Sneakers have specific names or nicknames, and they give a life and a personality to the object. Gill talks about three aspects to the rhetoric of trainer marketing as follows: (1) technological progress helps to enhance performance, (2) that would better the self physically and psychological, and (3) the aesthetics of sports shoe. Gill explains that the branding rhetoric of sports shoes is a compelling mix of performance, self-identity, and aesthetic concerns. Sneakers became an icon of global marketing power (Gill 2011: 371). Vanderbilt also writes:

> Sneaker names are generally meant to connote better performance in athletes. Speed, aggressiveness, aerodynamism, technical precision, prowess, intimidation, ruggedness, and physics-converting motions are the desired outcomes. Thus names like "Attack" and "React," "Carom" and "Kaboom," "Flight" and "Lightning." (Vanderbilt 1998: 64)

Similarly, the Air Jordan series have a motto every year which represents Jordan's athletic prowess, quick jumping ability, and competitive spirit that are transferred to those who wear the same shoes (see Table 3.1). The mottos indicate Jordan's high jumping ability, such as "Taking Flight" for AJ IV, "Choose Your Flight" for AJ 2012, and "Tailored for Flight" for AJ XX9 and imply his highest social status, such as "Pure Gold" for AJ VII, "The Dynasty Continues" for AJ XII, and "Performance Luxury" for AJ XX1.

Table 3.1 *Air Jordan Sneakers and Their Yearly Mottos (1984 to Present)*

Year released	Name	Motto
1984–1985	Air Jordan I	Notorious
1987	Air Jordan II	Italian Stallion
1988	Air Jordan III	Gotta be the Shoes
1989	Air Jordan IV	Taking Flight
1990	Air Jordan V	The Fighter
1991	Air Jordan VI	Promised Land
1992	Air Jordan VII	Pure Gold
1993	Air Jordan VIII	Strap In
1994	Air Jordan IX	Perfect Harmony
1995	Air Jordan X	The Legacy Continues
1996	Air Jordan XI	Class Act
1997	Air Jordan XII	The Dynasty Continues
1998	Air Jordan XIII	Black Cat Pounces

Year released	Name	Motto
1999	Air Jordan XIV	Race Reality
2000	Air Jordan XV	Speed Sound
2001	Air Jordan XVI	Marching On
2002	Air Jordan XVII	Jazzed Up
2003	Air Jordan XVIII	Last Dance
2004	Air Jordan XIX	Full Flex
2005	Air Jordan XX	Living Greatness
2006	Air Jordan XX1	Performance Luxury
2007	Air Jordan XX2	Hit the Afterburners
2008	Air Jordan XX3	The Number of Greatness
2009	Air Jordan 2009	Beyond
2010	Air Jordan 2010	Full Speed Ahead
2011	Air Jordan 2011	Be Quick Be Explosive
2012	Air Jordan 2012	Choose Your Flight
2013	Air Jordan XX8	Dare to Fly
2014	Air Jordan XX9	Tailored for Flight
2015	Air Jordan 30	TBA

Based on information sourced from www.cardboardconnection.com.

Gill explores the communicative rhetoric of the sneakers and its powerful hold on cultural meanings:

The release of a new model is able to invoke a passion among consumers so intense that they will spend large amounts of money and effort to acquire it. This is no "consumer madness" or irrational desire. A case must be made for fuller understanding of the powerful "rhetoric" of the sports shoe and the meanings it assumes for its owners, whether fans or collectors, wearers or nonwearers. (Gill 2011: 373)

The sneaker language consists of primarily action-oriented words which motivate the wearer to initiate action and be proactive.

The increasing significance of gender and the declining significance of race

During the First Wave pre-Jordan era, the sneaker subculture was indeed dominated by the minorities, especially the black boys and young men. Initially, the sneaker companies targeted the black hip-hop culture to cultivate the urban black market. Wearing a cool pair of sneakers was a status symbol of drug dealers and gangs, and the mainstream press was reporting that sneakers were drug dealers' fashion of choice that gangs were buying, and their shoes matched their gang colors (Vanderbilt 1998: 33). Michael Eric Dyson also writes: "the sneaker reflects at once the projection and stylization of black urban realities linked in our contemporary historical moment to rap culture and the underground political economy of crack, and reigns as the universal icon for the culture of consumption" (quoted in Vanderbilt 1998: 33).

However, as the sneaker phenomenon makes a huge turn after the Second Wave, I argue that the sneaker subculture is less about class and race than about gender and fashion. And because sneakers were part of rap musicians' informal dress code, many still associate the sneaker subculture to the particular racial group and talk about the racial divide within the sneaker subculture. Today, sneakers are as much a fashion item for minority youths as they are for mainstream white teenagers. By the mid-1990s, white teenagers became the primary consumers of hip-hop culture and fashion taking after and incorporating the black teens fashion and lifestyle. As Rebecca Robinson explains provocatively in her "It Won't Stop: The Evolution of Men's Hip-Hop Gear" (2008: 259): "The white audience 'weakened' the blackness of rap, making it easier for mainstream America to tolerate and adopt."

As early as 1978, William Julius Wilson wrote a controversial book "The Declining Significance of Race." He talked about the impact of industrialization on the changing patterns of race and class relations and analyzed the modern industrial period of race relations, giving particular attention to the role of structural changes in the economy and the political changes of the state in displacing racial antagonism from the economic sector to social, political, and community concerns and in creating vastly different mobility opportunities for different segments of the black population (Wilson 1978). He argued that race as a social factor is becoming less and less significant as industrialized societies become increasingly technological and those who can catch up with the development of technology will socially rise while those who do not will stay at the lower end of the social hierarchy, and one's social placement will no longer depend on one's racial background. The ability and the skill to use technology have provided much opportunities and greater life chances to the youths. They are learning a sneaker business at a young age and the entrepreneurial spirit through sneaker trading.

The construction of masculine identity

What is important in analyzing the youths' social behavioral patterns is how they acquire their subjective meaningful identities. As Stone writes (quoted in Roach-Higgins, Eicher and Johnson 1995: 23): "When one has identity, he is situated—that is, cast in the shape of a social object." It determines one's placement in a social context which inadvertently affects his behavior and thoughts. For sneaker enthusiasts, it is the type of sneakers that they put on their feet which in turn manifests their masculine identity and the level of fashion that they can achieve. Modernity allows people to have and experiment with multiple different identities. People change jobs, residence, families, even nationalities, lifestyles, and so on. Identities are not fixed but are always changing and moving, so we have to keep on going to grasp our identity which is a way to know our sense of self.

Theorists of fashion, such as Herbert Blumer (1969), Fred Davis (1992), and Diana Crane (2000), have emphasized the importance of expressing identities. We all have multiple identities, and each identity is projected through our outward appearance, and today, fashion is consumer-driven (Crane 2000). Fashion which used to be class based had shifted primarily to gender, but more recently, it is about many other choices of identities.

Identity, including gender, is a socially constructed notion. Colleen R. Callahan and Jo B. Paoletti in their article, "Is It a Girl or a Boy? Gender Identity and Children's Clothing" (2011), explain that in the nineteenth century, babies and young children, both boys and girls, dressed alike while adult attire was gender specific:

Babies and young children were considered innocents who, in their sexual immaturity, did not need specifically male or female clothing....Clothing modeled on female attire seemed proper for little boys because boys spent their first years within the feminine sphere of home and hearth, culturally and legally subordinate to men....Breeching, the occasion when a nineteenth century boy put away the skirts and dresses of baby hood and donned his first pair of trousers, was a significant event in his life. When a boy assumed that most exclusive element of male dress, trousers, society viewed him as symbolically beginning the process of becoming a man. The age at which a boy was breeched depended on parental influence. (Callahan and Paoletti 2011: 193)

Crane also explains how a man's identity construction through dress has changed over the years:

In comparison with the nineteenth century, late twentieth-century clothing codes are more complex. Nineteenth-century codes were primarily based on distinctions related to class and region. In cities, class codes were easy to recognize and interpret, although many people did not have the means to dress in the style of the middle class. Regional codes were irrelevant in cities, as were the codes governing the clothing of ethnic subgroups, whose members were generally immigrants and, consequently marginal. At the end of the twentieth century, clothes worn for different types of occupations are relatively easy to decipher.... However, the "street" is much more chaotic in its clothing codes than in the nineteenth century. Leisure clothes are more difficult than occupational clothes to read, because they are a vehicle of self-expression and a greater variety of codes is operating. (Crane 2000: 199)

One's identity may be strengthened and reinforced through his or her presence on social media through virtual communication and interaction. Society gives us identities, but at the same time, we try to attain that identity we aspire to. Haenfler succinctly points out:

Most of us have, at one time or another, dreamed of being someone we are not—maybe a movie star, professional athlete, revolutionary, or supermodel. Virtual worlds may help us live out these dreams as, in a sense, we can all be rich, powerful, and beautiful, even achieving a measure of fame. We have the opportunity to recreate and remake, to an extent, who we are.... All of these possibilities raise questions about how we think of our "self" and our identities. (Haenfler 2014: 117)

The Industrial Revolution in the eighteenth and the nineteenth centuries brought about massive changes in social structures, such as increasing democracy, social mobility, and the invention of science, as well as in people's lifestyle and ideologies, such as the values of individualism and the belief in rational thinking. As western societies further developed and reached the stage of the globalization and urbanization which celebrate diversity and multiculturalism, it resulted in creating multiple norms which we appreciate, and we respect and cherish different values, beliefs, attitudes, and norms. But the disadvantage of having too many choices in terms of values and norms is that people get confused and are not sure which ones to choose. From a Durkheimian perspective, that will put us in a state of anomie (see Chapter 5). As a result, the youths struggle to search for a group or a community to belong, and that provides them with a new set of norms and rules to follow, including how they dress, and that is one of the functions that subcultural affiliation and membership serves. Clark discusses some of the merits found in contemporary subcultures as follows:

It is often a temporary vehicle through which teens and young adults select a somewhat prefabricated identification, make friends, separate from their parents, and individuate themselves ... is heavily interactive with capitalist enterprise. Thus subcultures is both a discourse that continues to be a meaningful tool for countless people and, at the same time, something of a pawn of the culture industry. (Clark 2003: 227)

Based on the symbolic-interactionist theory, ambivalence in regard to one's outward appearance also affects the ambiguous and uncertain nature of one's definition of an identity (Davis 1992). With multiple roles to possess and perform, identities are diverse and fluid. They pick up an identity today and drop it the next day. This is an indication of a shallow level of attachment and commitment. It is allegedly common for a young person to choose a prefab subculture off the rack, wear it for a few years, and then rejoin with the "mainstream" culture that they never really left at all (Clark 2003: 224). Sneaker enthusiasts select the community that grants them a solid male identity that they want to hang on to in an age where gender identities are becoming fluid and flexible.

Conclusion

Boys and young men are attracted to sneakers because wearing the exclusive pair gives them a solid identity as a male in a society where identities are fluid and flexible. They feel that they are literally wearing masculinity on their feet. It also gives them a status, power, respect, and social acknowledgment from their peers. The race factor that used to be significant in the 1970s sneaker hunting is declining in its significance since the sneaker phenomenon is widely spreading to all ages, races, and classes. Many subcultures are gender-specific since that is a way to reproduce the gender divide between men and women. The sneaker community reinforces the structural element in maintaining male dominance over women. Sneakers continue to symbolize maleness and masculinity, and sneaker collection remains to be a male activity with an emphasis on speed and competition. Next chapter will explain how this footwear was transformed into a fashion object.

4
SNEAKERS AS FASHION: RECLAIMING MASCULINE ADORNMENT

Fashion and adornment have been a female affair and task since the Industrial Revolution. As Reilly and Cosbey write in the Introduction chapter of *Men's Fashion Reader*, there is a shortage of literature on the topic of men and dress since the subject of dress traditionally has not been considered "manly" in nature (2008: xi). Men often shy away from anything that exists in the female territory since it could label them as "feminine," which is the quality that the majority of men do not wish to possess. Fashion is too trivial a topic for men to be bothered with (Reilly and Cosbey 2008: xii).

But men also have a role in fashion as well, as McNeil writes:

> Fashion is considered as a complex social practice in which challenges to reform male appearances are sometimes made by figures with the power to expect obedience. Men have also used their appearance as a strategy of refusal or disinterest in the dominant culture that surrounds them. Others have been reformers who tried to convince the populace that their model of dress would lead to better social relationships. (McNeil 2009: 15)

The sneaker subculture is a community of boys and young men that is bounded by one item of dress which could potentially become a fashion item. They adorn and embellish their feet with the latest sneakers and are constantly chasing the more fashionable ones to compete with other fellow sneaker enthusiasts who are also male. All of the sneaker enthusiasts I have talked to and interviewed agree that it *is* a fashion item. But the practice of sneaker hunting and collection, although it is a practice of fashion, is not a female activity. At least for them, it is a male activity.

In this chapter, I discuss the complex and contradictory relationship between men and dress and also explore how a mundane object can be transformed into a sought-after fashion item. Sneakers are one of the best case studies to show the social transformation process of an object into fashion. Footwear is a tangible cultural object, while fashion is an intangible cultural idea and belief. Veblen in his *The Theory of Leisure Class* ([1899] 1957) talks about three principles of pecuniary culture, that is, conspicuous consumption, conspicuous waste, and conspicuous leisure. Fashion is surplus and excess. When a pair of sneakers goes beyond its practical functions, it becomes fashion.

In order for clothing to become fashion, it has to go through a systematic transformation (Kawamura 2005). Fashion is mostly associated with clothing because that is an item that changes constantly, repeatedly, and regularly. The content of fashion is never important, but it is the context that requires analytical attention and the investigation of the conversion process of a pair of athletic shoes into fashion (Kawamura 2005). The public expects clothing fashion to change but not footwear; however, the sneaker subculture shows that sneakers are indeed a fashion item, and the novelty and the scarcity of the products determine the status of a sneaker and the wearer. A Reebok marketing official says:

> We live in a world where consumer products can define, or at least be outward badges, of a person's character.... Somewhere along the line in their mercurial history, sneakers had gone from "once lowly" part-time shoes to "badges" of character; whether they were retro Puma Clydes on the feet of cutting-edge rock musician or politically useful "Made in the USA" New Balance on President Clinton. (Quoted in Vanderbilt 1998: 44)

Sneakers are no longer "lowly." Sneakers play a major part of fashion consumption influencing not only the footwear industry but also high fashion brands that are now producing high-priced sneakers, such as Comme des Garçons, Louis Vuitton, and Rick Owens, among many others. Comme des Garçons Play × Converse Pro Leather collection with the heart-with-eyes logo has been very popular among young boys (Plate 4.1). Back in 2009, Louis Vuitton collaborated with a popular rapper Kanye West and came up with a collection of sneakers with three models and ten color ways (Plate 4.2), which are still worn on the streets of New York. Rick Owens, an American designer, who shows his clothing collection in Paris and is also a creative director of Revillon, a French fur company, has his signature Geobasket sneaker collection (Plate 4.3). In 2014, an upscale American department store, Saks Fifth Avenue, opened a designer sneaker shop that sells sneakers designed by well-known fashion houses and designers, such as Balenciaga, Jimmy Cho, and Givenchy, among many others.

Plate 2.1 Custom-painted sneakers by @customkicksznj.

Plate 2.2 Custom-painted sneakers by @customkickznj.

Plate 2.3 Nike Air Jordan XX9.

Plate 2.4 Nike Air Jordan XIII Retro.

Plate 2.5 Nike Air Jordan XIII Retro.

Plate 2.6 Nike Air Max 90.

Plate 2.7 Nike Air Force One.

Plate 2.8 Nike Foamposite Pro Asteroid.

Plate 2.9 Nike Air Foamposite One Polarized Pink.

Plate 2.10 Nike Air Foamposite One Knicks.

Plate 2.11 Nike Total Air Foamposite Max Silver.

Plate 2.12 Nike Flyknit Racer.

Plate 2.13 Puma Disc Blaze Lite Tech.

Plate 3.1 Nike Air Foamposite Pro Spiderman.

Plate 3.2 adidas × Jeremy Scott JS Wings 2.0.

Plate 3.3 SneakerCon at Jacob Javits Convention Center in NY.

Plate 3.4 SneakerCon at Jacob Javits Convention Center in NY.

Plate 3.5 SneakerCon at Jacob Javits Convention Center in NY.

Plate 3.6 Nike LeBron X Classic.

Plate 3.7 Ewing 33 Hi Burgundy Suede.

Plate 3.8 Nike Air Jordan XIV Retro Ferrari.

Plate 3.9 Nike Zoom Kobe 6 Grinch Green Xmas.

Plate 4.1 Converse × Comme des Garçons.

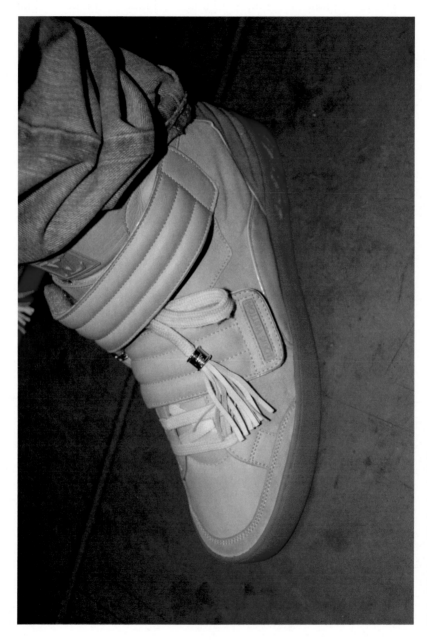

Plate 4.2 Kanye West × Louis Vuitton.

Plate 4.3 Rick Owens Geo Basket.

Plate 4.4 Nike Air Max LeBron Championship.

Plate 4.5 Staple x New Balance M577 "Black Pigeon".

Plate 4.6 Nike Kobe 9 EM Independence Day.

Plate 4.7 Nike What the Lebron 11.

Plate 4.8 Nike Air Jordan III.

Plate 4.9 Nike Air Jordan IX Retro Doernbecher.

Plate 4.10 Nike Air Jordan V Retro.

Plate 4.11 Nike KD VI Bamboo.

Plate 4.12 Nike Air Huarache LSR.

Plate 4.13 Nike LeBron XI Xmas.

Plate 4.14 adidas ZX Flux Multi Prism.

Plate 4.15 adidas Superstar.

Plate 4.16 Supreme × Comme des Garçons × Vans Sk 8.

Plate 4.17 Supreme × Air Force Foamposite One.

Plate 4.18 Supreme × Nike Air Force One.

A functional shift from practicality to adornment

As discussed in the previous chapters, when sneakers were first invented, their primary purpose and functions were comfort and practicality. For athletes, sneakers they wear must meet a certain standard of functionality so that they can achieve the highest performance possible whether it is basketball or skateboarding. What the athletes look for is the fit, the grip, and the comfort of the sneakers. After all, the first sneakers invented by Converse were to enhance the performance of a basketball player. They possessed no aesthetic components, and no one expected sneakers to be good-looking or fashionable.

FauxAmi, a skateboard exhibition organizer in Germany, explains the importance of shoes in skateboarding:

> Skateboarders have always paid a lot of attention to shoes. After all, they're what connect us to our boards — and to the world at large. Skaters know what difference a pair of shoes can make. We not only wear shoes — we UTILIZE them. We test them to the limits, wear them down, ski them across griptape and hot pavement. And when they're all beat up, we go to lengths to make them last a little bit longer, stand some more abuse, even when there's hardly any more sole left to walk on. We're an authority on which shoes have good grip and which shoes don't. We know which features make sense and which ones are just bells and whistles thrown on top for extra flair. We KNOW shoes, because we live in them. (Quoted in Blümlein et al. 2008: 12–13)

Doug Schneider, a professional skateboarder, also writes in his essay "Skate Shoes" about the elements he looks for when he buys a new pair of sneakers:

> Low tops often added mobility to the ankle while high tops provide more support and protection. Many people who use low tops wear ankle guards to protect the ankles. Most ankle guards restrict ankle movement to some degree, though less than wearing high top tennis shoes .... Next thing to consider is the material you want the tops to be made of. For instance, suede stretches a lot more than canvas. If you buy a suede show which fits perfect when you first buy it, it will tend to stretch out and you may end up having to wear two pairs of socks after a while .... Another important point is the relative advantage and disadvantage of soft (rubbery) soles as opposed to stiff soles .... Tread patterns vary greatly and do tend to affect grip. The more tread that touches the board, the better the grip .... Finally, when buying your shoes, check soles for loose glue joints, loose threads and imperfections on the bottom of the soles. (2008: 59)

Adornment and fashion have never been the primary concerns especially for serious athletes, and for those who are in sports, sneakers are a must item that should be selected with caution because what type of sneakers they wear affect their performance a great deal. These athletes automatically become shoe connoisseurs. Their choice of sneakers is not based on what they look like, but it is more about what they feel like when they wear them. It is all the technical aspects of the shoes that matter most for professional athletes.

However, during the Second Wave and the Third Wave Phenomenon, as sneakers became more and more commercialized in line with the personification of success through the sneakers that the professional athletes wear, the fashion and the adornment aspects of sneakers became increasingly important.

While it is always dangerous to overgeneralize causes or reasons of a phenomenon, those who are known as sneaker experts had more or less felt "deviant" or "different" or "unable to fit in" during their childhood, but then they realized that the aesthetic component of sneakers could attract others. One of the sneaker collectors in my interview said:

> I was always picked on in school. But one day I wore this particular type of sneakers, one of my classmates said to me "wow, that's cool" …. That's when I realized that something that I wear on my feet can attract people's attention in a positive way. That was an amazing experience and feeling. That's how I got hooked on sneakers.

Another sneaker enthusiast recounted a similar story:

> Once I started getting attention in school because of the sneakers I wear, I always wanted to wear cool sneakers. I think it's the attention and the recognition you get that makes you addicted to sneakers. Sneakers really boost your male ego. I feel cool. I feel confident.

Sneaker enthusiasts have more or less experienced a moment when they fell deeply in love with sneakers, and they remember exactly how and when their fascination started. Heard explains his first encounter in the early 1980s with sneakers that he was fascinated by:

> Stumbling through dark, cramped side streets on a grim, winter's afternoon, heading toward the hallowed turf of my local soccer ground, through the crowds of lads strutting as proud as peacocks I see them. The hit is immediate. Welcome, to the world of Trainer Obsession. There was something hypnotic about the whole package. The colours, the logo, the contrasting shiny nylon and suede materials—and later on, even the box, struck as cord deep within. These trainers were not just for wearing to run or kick in; they were more than

that. They were items of desire, beauty ... something I just had to possess. From that day on, trainers had taken a hold on me, and the grip is as strong today as it was way back then. (Heard 2003: 8)

Sneakers became a significant part of the youth culture, and as Gill explains (2011: 383), as the high-performance features of the trainer were taken up as essential equipment for everyday living, the gap between sportswear and fashion—once defined in opposition as functional uniforms versus stylish clothing—has been closing.

The male fascination with sneakers as a fashion object tells us that fashion is not just a female affair, as many had assumed. Reilly and Cosbey write:

In Western culture, we have grown accustomed to certain ways of thinking about men and their orientation toward appearance and dress ... we generally don't think of dress as "a man's subject." To be more specific, we assume that men are not particularly concerned about personal appearance, at least not to the extent that women are. As long as men appear to have met some basic standard of personal grooming, it seems they are satisfied with the way they look. It follows, then, that men are also generally believed to be uninterested in fashion. Traditional thinking has placed fashion in the domain of women. (Reilly and Cosbey 2008: xii)

The intense pursuit of sneaker fashion by men proves otherwise. Their ambition and enthusiasm for the latest sneakers are comparable to women's everlasting passion for beauty and fashion. There is also a false belief that men's fashion does not exist (Reilly and Cosbey 2008: xiii). Many of the fashion and dress scholars have overlooked men's feet. Men's fashion has been subtle, covert, and underplayed because overt self-display and self-adornment are indeed believed to be "very feminine," but that belief and attitude are changing dramatically. Men are reclaiming adornment and fashion that they once had and were forced to abandon and to adopt a business suit as if it was their uniform since the Industrial Revolution. Men's passion for fashion is beginning to resurface, and it is reclaiming its domain as exclusively male. They are literally wearing "masculinity on their feet" (Plates 4.4–4.7).

Sneaker enthusiasts are one of the most fashionable groups of people as they always decide what to wear on their feet everyday before they decide which clothes to wear. Their fashion literally starts from bottom-up which is symbolical of their fashion diffusion process, the bubble-up or trickle-up theory of fashion which Herbert Blumer and other scholars after him had argued. For Blumer (1969), fashion is directed by consumer taste, and it is a fashion designer's task to predict and read the modern taste of the collective mass, and he situates consumers in the construction of fashion.

Reclaiming fashion and adornment as a male affair

Studies on historical male costume indicate that men of the upper class were extremely fashionable and cared about their appearance. At different times in western history, men's fashion has been decorative, impractical, erotic, changeable, revolutionary, idealistic, oppressive, and restrictive, subject to strict protocols, and laden with meaning (Reilly and Cosbey 2008: 3).

Lois Banner in her article "The Fashionable Sex, 1100–1600" (2008: 6–16) examines the male body and male fashion in late medieval and early modern Europe. There was the emphasis on parts of the body associated with sexuality in the late eleventh century with the adoption of elongated, pointed shoe styles, and that continued until the fourteen century with short jacket, long legs, and the exposure of the genitals, and furthermore, men's dress became feminized with the periodic addition to decorative softening features (2008: 7). From the mid-fourteenth century until the mid-eighteenth century, male dress of the upper class was decorative, flamboyant, and colorful with a lot of details and trimmings just like female dress. Boucher explained that whereas men in pre-eighteenth-century Europe were as, or more, splendidly dressed than women, in the eighteenth century women surpassed in rich clothing (1987).

A male fashion icon: Beau Brummel

In her "Dandyism, Visual Games, and the Strategies of Representation," Olga Vainshtein writes: "The dandyism of the English Regency period established the models of self-fashioning that became stereotypes of men's behavior in society during the nineteenth century" (Vainshtein 2009: 84).

George Byan Brummel (1778–1840), a British military officer, famously known as "Beau Brummel" remains in the history of western fashion as a male fashion icon and a "dandy." He is described as having a distinguished bearing, dignity of manner, cool self-possession, and a pleasing voice. He had good humor, wit, and a tongue that was often caustic (Parker in Brummel [1932] 1972: x).

Eleanor Parker writes about Brummel's background in the Introduction ([1932] 1972: vii–xviii): "his father, William Brummel, as intimate friend and confidential adviser, as well as private secretary, to the Prime Minister, Lord North, and from infancy throughout his life, Beau Brummel was accustomed to the society of cultured people."

He was known as a tastemaker, trendsetter, and an influencer of men's fashion. While he was still at the University of Oxford, he joined the army and became a coronet in the Prince of Wale's own regiment. He became very close to the prince, who later became King George IV, and his circle of friends who all dressed well. By 1798, he was already a favorite of the prince and his fellow officers, and from this time, until his flight from England in 1816, he wielded a dominating influence over the most exclusive group of British society—a group known as the one of the most brilliant in the history of England (Parker in Brummel [1932] 1972: ix–x). Brummell was a member of an old Tory club White's, one of the few closed and highly prestigious clubs with limited membership (Vainshtein 2009). Parker explains his tight network within the aristocratic community:

> His friends were not merely the fashionable idlers, but the most intellectual men of the day. His word was law on dress and manners. Even after his fall from royal favor, he continued to be fashion's arbiter and retained his following. It is significant that among those who remained his friends were members of the Prince of Wales's family. (Parker in Brummel [1932] 1972: x).

Around 1800, he earned a nickname "Beau" because of his elegant and impeccable style, and men listened to his fashion advice. Brummel was the outstanding authority on the subject. He could make something into fashion although his extravagant lifestyle put him into enormous debt later in his life. He had influenced the meaning of masculinity in the beginning of the nineteenth century. "Brummel was the first to invent a very important and modern principle of vestimentary behavior, the principle of 'conspicuous inconspicuouness.' It meant the imperative of dressing elegantly, yet unobtrusively, without attracting undesirable attention" (Vainshtein 2009: 94).

Beau Brummel was an arbiter of a sophisticated taste and refinement.[1] Vainshtein explains that newly ordered visual games were part of social codes and models of representation introduced by the British dandies. "The fashionable people of the Regency looked at one another as though looking in a mirror, having taken pleasure in and convinced themselves of the weight and reality of the body as a visible thing" (Vainshtein 2009: 85).

Negative views of dandy

There has been much prejudice and discrimination against men, including Beau Brummel, who are into fashion. Michael Carter explains how European scholars, such as Thomas Carlyle, a British philosopher, and Thornstein Veblen, an American economist, looked at dandy:

> Carlyle sees Dandies as almost pathological figures whose obsession with their appearance places them at a tangent to most "normal" men. As far as Veblen ([1899] 1957) is concerned, the dandy is distinguishable only by the *degree and intensity* with which his appearance incorporates economic and social principles already at work in the male population at large. (Carter 2003: 47)

Georg Simmel, a German sociologist, also points out that women, and not men, were strong adherents to fashion and the female quality of fashion:

> If fashion gives expression to the impulse towards equalization and individualization, as well as to the allure of imitation and conspicuousness, this perhaps explains why it is that women, broadly speaking, adhere especially strongly to fashion. (Simmel [1905] 1997: 196)

S.A.M. Adshead in his *Material Culture in Europe and China, 1400–1800* (1997) also points out that fashion is a type of female intelligence and practice in the West. Therefore, western dress history indicates that self-display and concerns for beauty had shifted from a male task to a female task. Men used to be "more ornamental and decorative than the female" in appearance, but a profound reorganization of masculinity took place in the late eighteenth and nineteenth centuries (Flügel 1930). With the Industrial Revolution, overall societal values, male values in particular, transformed dramatically. Ever since the feminization of fashion, self-display has been believed to be a female affair.

Men abandoned sartorial decorations, that is, fashion, and adopted less flamboyant, subdued colors and simplified silhouettes, such as a traditional male suit. According to Flugel (1930: 110–111), men may be said to have suffered a great defeat in the sudden reduction of male sartorial decorativeness which took place at the end of the eighteenth century, and they abandoned their claim to be considered beautiful. He named this dramatic shift "The Great Masculine Renunciation" (Flügel 1930), which states that men gave up fashion, adornment, and self-adornment, and concerns for outward appearance were left up to women. It has more or less remained a standard male uniform. Decorating oneself was no longer part of the male domain, although it was still an expression of "conspicuous consumption." Men of higher social standing would use fashion as a tool to show off their wealth vicariously through their women, such as wives, daughters, and mistresses, and used them as a vehicle in the display of wealth since men could no longer flaunt their wealth through their decorative and flamboyant outward appearance (Simmel [1905] 1997; Veblen [1899] 1957).

Sneaker obsession as street dandyism

This idea that fashion is a female task has remained hegemonic for a few centuries, but sneaker enthusiasts are changing this back to what it used to be. Fashion can blatantly be a male affair, and exclusive sneakers are a symbol of a social status, wealth, and power. Sneaker enthusiasts are like the modern-day Beau Brummel who takes care of his physical appearance obsessively.

Nathaniel Adams in his *I Am Dandy: The Return of the Elegant Gentleman* (2013) explains the modern version and interpretation of a dandy in today's society as follows:

> There is something of the obsessive-compulsive, the narcissistic, and the tragic about this condition and the various forms it takes: these are men who simply couldn't exist any other way. The true dandies aren't selling anything; for them clothing isn't a job—it's a divinely-ordained vocation to which they have been called by some unseen force. These are the men who, stranded alone on a desert island, would still dress up every day, using fish bones as tie pins and polishing their shoes with squid ink. They're complete package: clothes, surroundings, personality, behavior, taste, all working in concert to achieve a desired effect. (Adams 2013: 8)

They are all possessed by a sometimes ruinous and romantic obsession with appearance, particularly in matters of dress and deportment (Adams 2013: 10), and such intensity and passion parallel with sneaker enthusiasts, although they never wear a Savile Row suit with a tie or lace-up Ferragamo shoes. They have their own definition of "dressing well" with the right sneakers.

Andrew Yamato defines today's dandy as follows:

> The key is to make clothing an end in itself. The best dressers aren't concerned with the power or prestige or sex appeal that good togs might confer; they genuinely love clothes for their own sake, wearing them with care and confidence, without ostentation or shame. That kind of unapologetic authenticity is the real stuff of masculinity; it's never lost its power to impress, and more importantly, its every bit as much fun as it ever was. (Yamato quoted in Adams 2013: 9)

They are reclaiming fashion, but to avoid being "effeminate," girls and women are shut out from the community.

Informal norms of sneaker fashion

On the limited upper space of the shoe, sneaker enthusiasts experiment and play with various creative ways to express their identity. Participants in the subculture express, promote, and affirm their membership by adopting distinct styles. How they wear their sneakers symbolizes a set of values that unites its members. Paul Willis (1978) explains that style is symbolic of subcultural values and subcultures' relationship to the mainstream. In the world of dandies, the role of signifying detail as a decisive semiotic message also corresponded to the idea of "conspicuous inconspicuousness," and a visual message could be encoded through the careful folds of starched neckcloth, a plain but stylish ring, or blackening the soles of the boots (Vainshtein 2009: 94).

Similarly, sneaker enthusiasts are also bonded by their informal norms, such as the subtle and sometimes complex dos and don'ts of how to wear and maintain sneakers in the right way. Every subculture has its own values and norms, and a sneaker subculture is no exception.

For instance, white sneakers must remain spotless and immaculate[2] (Plates 4.8–4.10). That is a sign that you are a "true sneakerhead." There was a time when sneaker enthusiasts carried around toothbrushes in case someone treaded on them, and if the sneakers got dirty, then they could clean them immediately with the toothbrush. The sneakers should look like as if they were just bought and taken out of the box. This applies how Veblen explained fashion:

> It will be in place, by way of illustration, to show in some detail how the economic principles so far set forth apply to everyday facts in some direction of the life process. For this purpose no line of consumption affords a more apt illustration than expenditure on dress…. Elegance dress serves its purpose of elegance not only in that it is expensive, but also because it is the insignia of leisure. It not only shows the wearer is able to consume a relatively value, but it argues at the same time that he consumes without producing. (Veblen [1899] 1957: 171)

He talked about elegance in men's dress. Elegance for him meant "neat and spotless garments." Whiteness in dress or sneakers is a symbol of leisure and status. The sneaker enthusiasts also try to avoid making creases on the sneaker. There is a gadget called a "decreaser" that is placed inside the shoe so that the upper shape of a shoe stays in tact, or they wear a pair or two pairs of thick socks.

Shoe laces are also an important element and are part of the informal code for sneaker fashion (Plates 4.11–4.14). Garcia talks about "The No No's of New York Sneaker Culture" (2003: 226–228). Laces should not be so tight that the sides of the support touch together (Sake quoted in Garcia 2003: 226); laces should be washed constantly so that they are not dirty (Fabel quoted in Garcia 2003: 226); and colored laces were out unless they were candy-striped (Jonny Snakeblack Fever quoted in Garcia 2003: 226). These informal norms and code originate from the streets and are accepted by the insider fans.

Sneaker enthusiasts began to customize and experiment with different types, widths, and colors of shoes laces and the way the laces are tied. Sneakers are often sold with two or three pairs of shoelaces in different colors so that the wearer can choose their laces as they wish, probably matching their socks, pants, and shirts. Hal Petersons writes:

> Before Chucks were manufactured in a variety of colors besides black or white, chucks wearers would often substitute different colored shoelaces to

personalize their chucks…. The best athletic laces are the stretchable flat tubular laces that came with every pair of chucks until around 1990 when they were replaced with ribbed single layer laces in a cost-cutting move. Besides the standard flat or tubular models, shoelaces often come in extra-wide (flat) widths; in different weaves like rainbow or red, white and blue; in narrow round models like you see on many running shoes; in reversible two-color models; and in print patterns with checkered squares or other symbols. (Peterson 2007: 88)

One's interests in sneakers lead to the deeper understanding of all the details, including different types of laces and the construction, technology, and the fabric of the shoes.

In pursuit of limited edition sneakers: Neophilias and neomanias

While the clothing fashion industry is revolving at a very fast pace with several collections a year, no field in the fashion industry is as fierce, rapid, and competitive as the sneaker industry and sneaker consumption. There are new releases and launches almost every other day communicated through tweets and Instagram updates. If fashion is all about novelty, nothing can be newer than sneakers. As many of the collectors said to me, "It's important to be 'fresh.'"

As the sneaker subculture began to expand widely, there needed to be a strategy to make some social differences among the sneaker fans. One way to claim a status and gain respect from their peers was to find and buy limited edition sneakers. Some of them camp outside a store for a few days waiting for the release of an exclusive pair. There have been some incidents where a riot occurred among those who were eager to buy the new pair. There are no limits as to how far they would go or do to get the most recent limited editions.

In February 2005, when a new pair of limited edition sneaker called "Nike Pigeon Dunk" was released and sold at Reed Space, a boutique in Downtown New York, hundreds of young men lined up a few days in the cold before the release date, and the situation became so chaotic that there was almost a riot, and the NY police showed up. The incident was on the front page of *New York Post* the next day. More recently, on December 29, 2011, more than a hundred would-be buyers waited in line for hours outside a Foot Locker store at New York's Herald Square for the launch of the latest Air Jordan, AJ Retro 11 Concord which was $180 a pair (Mattioli 2011). The original black-and-white shoe was sold in 1996. Sneaker collectors were waiting hours before stores opened, and there were reports of scuffles, and the police had to be summoned in some cities.

Novelty is a crucial part of fashion, and it is a highly valued concept in fashion. Koenig refers to ardent fashion followers as "neophilia" (1973: 77) stating that humankind receptiveness for anything new is, among many other aspects, in some way essential to fashion-oriented behavior (Koenig 1973: 76). Similarly, Roland Barthes correlated fashion to newness as follows:

> Fashion doubles belongs to all the phenomena of neomania which probably appeared in our civilization with the birth of capitalism: in an entirely institutional manner, the new is a purchased value. But in our society, what is new in Fashion seems to have a well-defined anthropological function, one which derives from its ambiguity: simultaneously unpredictable and systematic, regular and unknown. (Barthes 1967: 300)

Veblen also explains novelty as an element of fashion (1964: 72): "The requirement of novelty is the underlying principle of the whole of the difficult and interesting domain of fashion. Fashion does not demand continual flux and change simply because that way of doing is foolish; flux and change and novelty are demanded by the central principle of dress-conspicuous waste."

Furthermore, Koenig (1973: 76) writes: "although the contents of fashion are always a manifestation of their epoch, its structural form as a special kind of the controlled behavior incorporates certain constants which decide initially what fashion is." Change and novelty are the two characteristics that fashion encompasses, and institutions encourage and control the changes in style on a regular basis which simultaneously creates novelty; contents of fashion, that is clothing, are constantly changing, but fashion as a form always remains (Kawamura 2005: 6).

There is an obsessive desire for the new exclusive sneakers among the members. Sneakers should never look old and worn out. The evident correlation between the limited edition and its price is explained as follows:

> The limited nature of some of these releases can create sneakers with a near-mythical status, like the Nike Dunkle Low ... or the JB Classics MOTUG shoes on .... The rarest and most sought-after shoes can sky rocket in value, and these shoes are often only available in specific locations, they frequently crop up in online auctions with generously inflated price tags.... Where sports brands once looked to athletes to add credibility and desirability to their products, they now look to artists and designers. (Intercity 2008: 7–8)

These limited editions are now being controlled by sneaker companies and retailers. There are many releases of retro shoe models, and the collaborative limited edition shoes are often based on the safety of the manufacturers' best-selling models. According to Bengtson:

It made acquiring vintage sneakers from anywhere in the world as easy as a click of the mouse, and suddenly anyone with a computer and a bank account could build up a massive sneaker collection spanning all eras in a matter of days. The diggers were still out there … but spots were drying up, as savvy retailers realized that their old stock was worth more than the new. (Bengtson 2013: 89)

In order to maintain the sneaker subculture, someone or some companies must provide new sneakers so that they constantly have new information to share, exchange, and mobilize as a group and buy new pairs. A sneaker retailer says:

These days, the sneaker competition is all about hype. The companies purposely create a hype saying that new editions that are coming out are limited and exclusive. And young kids go berserk believing that if they get hold of that shoe, they can be "cool," and their friends will look up to them. They have no idea if that new shoe is good or bad or worth spending money on. They just go after the hype. But you know what? It's great for the industry.

The sneaker community calls them the "hypebeasts," which comes from one of the most popular websites for young men's contemporary fashion and streetwear, including sneakers, called Hypebeast (www.hypebeast.com) based in Hong Kong. It boasts more than 450,000 visitors a day and 14 million per month. Eugene Kan, former managing director of Hypebeast, who was at the company when I interviewed him but left in May 2015, explains the success of the website in my email interview as follows:

I'd like to think Hypebeast's ability to strike a chord is part passion and part critical eye. That critical eye is a bit hard to describe and I wouldn't say it's an innate ability as much as it is a by-product of always looking to learn and engage in new interesting cultural movements …. At the end of the day, our interest or ethos lies in … celebrating creativity and offering a platform for discovery …. We are extremely grateful that people find our interests captivating.

In choosing brands and items to post on their website which many of the youths believe are all "cool" products, Kan explains his selection criteria and standard:

I try not to be too methodical or scientific about it … seems to make it less organic. There are aspects of the business that benefit from automation but I'd like to think picking content is not one of them. I try to assess the presentation, that is probably one of the most important aspects of the content …. For example a product has negative repercussions for both site and brand when a product is not presented properly, as the site's aesthetic suffers and the brand is not presented in the best light. When it comes to the actual assessment, it's a balance between what we personally feel is cool and what the reader enjoys.

Visual aesthetics are important everywhere: how a product is presented or how one wears sneakers. They buy new sneakers, wear them, take pictures of them, and post them online to make sure their friends and peers know about it. The number of followers and likes are received as social acceptance and recognition as if they cannot attain them elsewhere. Kan objectively sees the negative side of the technology-dependent youths:

> The youth of today are wanting to create their own history book, and social media empowers them to do that. But as we also grow up in a world of social media, the currency becomes different. Followers, likes and retweets are not championed, and I feel that it can have some devastating consequences as people look to game the institution in hopes of acquiring fame and popularity which seems to be a central goal to some. I've always wondered, but never been able to back up my suspicion that the current way family life was playing out had the youth resort to their own means to become socialized and appreciated.

During my research, I was not able to find out each sneaker fan's social or family background, which would require an enormous amount of time and trusting relationship and friendship with each one of them, but as Kan suggests, it could possibly explain the current youth behavior, including obsessive sneaker hunting, to a certain extent.

The Third Wave Sneaker Phenomenon: Sneaker hunting as a game

As indicated earlier in Chapter 3, I have divided the sneaker phenomenon into three stages/waves: (1) The First Wave pre-Jordan era, (2) The Second Wave post-Jordan era, and (3) The Third Wave, which shares much of the characteristics of the Second Wave but are more intensified in terms of speed and competition.

The collectors during the First Wave valued being underground, and they were the pioneers who are still very much respected by their peers. But the current-day collectors value the exclusivity and fashion components of sneakers, and the value of fashion is determined by its scarcity. The Third Wave involves the use of social media as a tool of communication, and it is literally a minute-by-minute interaction in exchanging and acquiring the latest sneaker news. When you find someone's blog without any images, you are more likely to get bored and quickly move to someone else's. If pictures do not load quickly, you get impatient and log out.

Sneaker hunting itself has become a sports game that produces winners and losers. Garcia explains his long-time yearning to get a coolest pair of sneakers as a young child but soon realizes that there are those who are cooler than him in the sneaker competition:

I had Super Pro-Keds in blue canvas. I'll never forget what that felt like. It was a coming of age. I literally walked out of the store, got to the sidewalk, and burst into an all-out sprint.... The moment of glory was short-lived. The next week I saw my boy with Pro-Ked 60'ers that I'd never seen before. I was taken aback. I thought I was cool, but he was cooler. He was a step ahead. By getting my first pair of Super Pro-Keds I was just trying to fit in, but seeing the 69'ers made me realize immediately that I didn't want to just wear popular brands, I wanted to wear the coolest brands and models too. Envy is one of the seven deadly sins, and the easiest way to avoid it is to always be ahead of everyone in the sneaker game.... That took funds and license to hunt outside your neighborhood, neither of which I had until '80 when I got my first job. (Garcia 2003: 16)

Men are bonded through activities, while women are bonded through sharing emotions. The male bond is created through tasks and activities, and communication through social media has become more than a communication tool. Competitions in the male world are black and white, either they win or they lose. And it is often about the speed which is an essential factor in competition. Especially in sports, you win because you are fast, or you lose because you are too slow. Everything is black and white in men's perspectives. Basketball is about how fast you shoot your ball in the net. Cars are also about speed. Expensive cars run fast. Winners reach the goal first. And this competition factor through activities is a way to construct the unity and the bond among men. Men rarely sit down and share their feelings and emotions with their peers.

Although the sneaker enthusiasts compete in the sneaker hunting process, they have high regards for one another. They exchange and share information about sneakers, show off new sneakers that they bought, post them online, and nonverbally acknowledge those who are part of the same subculture.

Many of them also frequent fashion forums, such as NikeTalk, Hypebeast, StyleForum, and Superfuture, where they discuss different styles, looks, and designer labels over various threads. They also post pictures of their recent purchases and what they are wearing, indicated as "WAYWT" (which stands for What Are You Wearing Today), after their thread in Superfuture. There is the shoe edition of WAYWT. Similar to "likes" on Instagram, there is an option to "rep" (positive) and "neg" (negative) a member's post. These posters seek approval of or opinions for their styles to see if they are following the trends correctly or if they are putting together an outfit in a cool and fashionable way. Buying good clothing and having the right look become almost an obsession.

The love and passion for and obsession with sneakers that they share establishes camaraderie among the male youth, and there is the undeniable emotional attachment and involvement that they feel by being part of the community, and that is how they assert and reconfirm hegemonic masculinity that is perpetuated through their socialization process.

Technology allows us to spread our knowledge, messages, and information as widely as we wish, but at the same time, it has become difficult to guard our information as confidential. Technology has accelerated democratization and at the same time diminished a sense of exclusivity. Because exclusivity is difficult to maintain, it becomes even more desired today. The age of sneaker enthusiasts is becoming younger and younger, and sneaker hunting and collection are popular practices among junior high school and high school male students. As they get older, the object of a status symbol may be upgraded to cars, electronics, and houses all of which represent wealth, prestige, and power. They were quick to adopt smartphones and social media tools. One of the sneaker collectors says: "If you send a tweet to someone, and he doesn't respond to you for an hour, that's way too late! You are supposed to respond within four or five minutes or even less! If you are in this sneaker game, your responses should be quick!"

The commodification and diffusion of sneaker subculture

Commodity-oriented subcultures have become a billion-dollar industry. Bare skin, odd piercings, and blue jeans are not a source of moral panics these days: they often help to create new market opportunities, and they may serve a useful function for capitalism by making stylistic innovations that can then become vehicles for new sales (Clark 2003: 229). As a result, radical subcultural groups, such as hippies, punks, and gays, use consumer goods to declare their differences, and the code becomes comprehensible to the rest of the society and gets assimilated within a large set of cultural categories (McCracken 1988: 133). Similarly, as Frederic Jameson (1983: 124) explains, there is very little in either the form or the content of contemporary art that contemporary society finds intolerable and scandalous, and the most offensive forms are all taken in stride by society. Furthermore, Clark points out that, by the early 1970s, with commodification in full swing, some artists said to have compromised their integrity by becoming rich stars, and with "rock" having been integrated into the mainstream, some people felt that youth subcultures were increasingly a part of the intensifying consumer society, rather than opponents of the mainstream (2003: 225).

In my previous study on the French fashion system (2004), I treated fashion as an institutionalized system which offers the theoretical underpinnings of fashion-ology and explains how fashion can be studied empirically as an institution or an institutionalized system, and there are individuals related to fashion, including designers and many other fashion professionals, who engage in activities collectively, share the same belief in fashion, and participate together in producing and perpetuating not only the ideology of fashion but also fashion culture which is sustained by the continuous production of "fashion" (Kawamura 2005: 39). This idea can also be applied to fashion which derives from the subculture. Without any institutional support, a subculture remains marginal, unknown, and hidden. Similar to the Japanese youths, some subcultures have spread widely because each of them had the institutional cooperation and involvement, such as events, retailers, magazines, newspapers, websites, and blogs, among many others (Kawamura 2012).[3]

One or two stores are not enough to make a group of fans or followers an established subculture – at the same time, those who prefer to be part of the subcultures are often not in favor of mainstream tastes, beliefs, or lifestyles. The members enjoy the process of searching and looking for a one-of-a-kind item that no one else has or is wearing. The ironical contradiction is that subcultures are supposed to be marginal, but as the members begin to exchange information about the community and about themselves using social media, the sense of exclusivity is diminished or disappeared. In order for a subculture to have a strong presence, it needs to be widely diffused through the media, retailers, and celebrities.

New subcultures do not grow or expand commercially unless there are institutional supports to respond to consumer demands. Now that the sneaker subculture is spreading far and wide, it is the sneaker companies, to some extent, that take charge of the sneaker trend. No one goes around the stores, asking the salespeople to show them the back storage where they keep old sneakers, and try to discover unknown sneakers.

In February 2015, a new sneaker called Yeezy 750 Boost, a collaboration between Kanye West and adidas, was first launched in New York. The news created a buzz and hype among the collectors who are eager to find out when it will be released worldwide. Whenever the industry produces an exclusive edition, it wets the sneaker collectors' appetite, and this is a way to expand the subculture through commodification and commercialization. Sneakers are consumed as a material and an immaterial cultural object by the members. Consumption is an important part of subcultural experience in creating a subcultural identity.

Sneakers in music and movies

As Böse explains (2003: 170), it is the global resources of a cultural industry that has enabled (sub)cultural symbols and practices—from old, school trainers to body piercings, from bindis to tattoos—to spread increasingly quickly across the world. It could also be argued that the culture industry appropriates subcultural imagery as marketable and commercial:

> Early punks were too dependent on music and fashion as modes for expression; these proved to be easy targets for corporate cooptation.... Tactically speaking, the decisive subcultural advantage in music and style—their innovation, rebellion, and capacity to alarm—was preempted by the new culture industry, which mass-produced and sterilized punk's verve. (Clark 2003: 227)

There is no doubt about a strong and an inseparable correlation between rap music and sneakers. Sneakers are found in the music scene. Hip-hop culture with rap music that came out of New York in the 1970s expressed the youths' anger, disillusionment, and frustration toward the authorities and the establishment through their music which gave them a voice. It was an emotional outlet for them when they had nowhere else to turn to. The hip-hop culture combines rap music, DJ-ing, break-dancing, and street art, such as graffiti, and sneakers as part of their dress code. They gradually developed a style of their own with sagging jeans and oversized T-shirts with big logos. Their outfit matched their sneakers which were an indispensable part of their look. When hip-hop culture became a source of fashion ideas in the mid-to late 1980s, the spotless, untied sneaker was consolidated as a must-have style icon to finish a look consisting of oversized jeans and tracksuits (Gill 2011: 383).

Members of Run DMC, a popular rap group, had been wearing adidas Superstar (Plate 4.15) for sometime when they decided to release a song called "My adidas." This is another significant collaboration that brought the hidden sneaker subculture to the surface for the general public to see and notice. "My adidas" and Run DMC were crossover acts, key players in the movement of hip-hop out of the "ghetto" and into the boutique. They were among the first to promote a brand as part of their "brand"; today one can hardly find a hip-hop star who is not selling a fully accessorized look along with the music (Miller 2013: 149). This song led to a million-dollar contract between Run DMC and adidas, which was so successful that other sneaker companies followed suit and collaborated with rap musicians. Sneakers have appeared in countless hip-hop songs since then.[4] With the widespread popularity of hip-hop culture around the world, it also influenced the British punk rock music scene (Lv and Huiguang

2007: 237–238) as well as the grunge music scene in the 1990s, and they shed light on sneakers, such as the Converse All Star, since Nirvana's Kurt Cobain was always wearing them. When he was found dead, he was wearing black Converse sneakers.

Karaminas explains that the relationship between popular music, identity, and fashion is a symbiotic one:

> The fashion industry designs and *creates* garments, while popular music sells a *lifestyle* (aided by pop and rock stars), through the consumption of fashionable merchandise. Fashion and style are the visual counterparts to musical expression—the pose, the "look" merge to create a subcultural spectacle that is coopted by the mainstream via tastemakers, journalists, trend forecasters, fashion buyers, and so on. Businesses often seek to capitalize on the subversive allure of subcultures in search of *cool*, which is valuable in selling any product to a youth consumer. (Karaminas 2009: 349)

Sneakers have also appeared in a number of movies and played a significant role which helped create an image of the particular type of sneakers (see Table 4.1). It was an expansive promotional effort for the sneakers, which created a trend for a particular type of sneaker. In 1982, a movie, *Ridgemont High School*, which was about youngsters in Southern California made Vans slip-ons a popular item. Amy Hackerling, director of the movies, explains how it came about:

> Sean Penn, who played Jeff Spicoli, brought in the checkered Vans slip-ons himself, and I really liked them. I grew up back East during an era where everyone wore white sneakers, and I just loved how Vans looked. They were so different than what I was used to seeing, and they had so much personality. When Sean showed me the shoes for his costume, I trusted his judgment. (Amy Hackerling quoted in Palladini 2009: 130)

In the early 1980s, Vans did not market their sneakers. The only advertising they did was in skate magazines. But after this movie, they became famous nationwide. Everyone wanted to be cool like Spicoli, the character in the movie.

In Spike Lee's first movie *She's Gotta Have It* (1986), Lee himself plays a character Mars Blackmon who is an unemployed guy obsessed about sneakers, and he never takes them off. The appearance of Michael Jordan's AJ 1 sneakers is believed to be one of the contributing factors for the success of Jordan sneakers. In addition, Air Jordan IV had a role in Lee's another movie *Do the Right Thing* (1989). AJ IV is one of the most popular models in the Jordan series that its retro version was released several times in slightly different designs and colorways.

Table 4.1 *Sneakers in Movies*

Year	Name of movies	Sneakers
2010	*Game of Death*	Onitsuka Tiger Tai Chi
2010	*Robin Hood: Men in Tights*	Reebok Pump Omni Zone
2005	*School Daze game*	Nike AJ II
2005	*Sin City*	Converse Chuck Taylor
2004	*A Life Aquatic*	adidas Zissou
2004	*IRobot*	Converse Chuck Taylor
2003	*Lost in Translation*	Nike Air Woven
2002	*Shottas*	Nike AJ XII
2002	*In Blood Work*	Converse Chuck Taylor
2001	*One Night at Mac Cruise*	Converse Chuck Taylor
2000	*The Crimson Rivers*	Nike Air Jordan IV Retro
1998	*He Got Game*	Nike Air Jordan VIII
1997	*George of the Jungle*	Nike Air More Uptempo
1996	*Space Jam*	Nike Air Max Triax
1995	*The Cure*	Converse Chuck Taylor
1994	*Forrest Gump*	Nike Cortez
1994	*Clerks*	Asics Gel Saga II
1993	*The Skateboard Kid*	Converse Chuck Taylor
1992	*White Men Can't Jump*	Nike Air Command Force
1992	*Juice*	Reebok Pump Twilight Zone
1992	*Mo' Money*	Nike AJ VI
1991	*Boyz n the Hood*	Nike Air Flow
1991	*King Ralph*	Nike Air Max 9 0
1991	*New Jack City*	adidas Phantom Hi
1989	*Back to the Future II*	Nike Air Mag
1989	*Do the Right Thing*	Nike AJ IV

Year	Name of movies	Sneakers
1989	*Batman*	Nike Air Trainer III
1989	*See no Evil Hear no Evil*	Nike Air Pegasus ACG
1989	*Lean on Me*	Nike Air Max 87
1989	*Warlock*	Nike AJ II
1989	*Leviathan*	Nike Air Max 87
1989	*Gleaming the Cube*	Converse Chuck Taylor
1988	*Big*	Nike Air Force II
1988	*High Hopes*	Nike Orange Flame
1988	*Running on Empty*	Converse Chuck Tyalor
1988	*Working Girl*	adidas classic
1987	*Police Academy 4*	Nike Air Jordan 1
1987	*The Witches of Eastwick*	Nike Dunk Low
1986	*She's Gotta Have It*	Nike AJ 1
1986	*Slushin'*	Converse Chuck Taylor
1985	*Back to the Future*	Nike Vandal
1985	*The Goonies*	Nike Terra T/C
1985	*The Last Dragon*	Converse Chuck Taylor
1985	*The Breakfast Club*	Nike Internationalist
1985	*Heavy Weights*	Nike Air Huarache Light
1985	*Teen Wolf*	adidas Tourney
1985	*Back to the Future*	Converse Chuck Taylor
1984	*Beat Street*	Puma Suede
1984	*Beverley Hills Cop*	adidas Country
1984	*The Terminator*	Nike Vandal
1984	*Breakin'*	Nike Blazer
1984	*Police Academy*	adidas Summit
1982	*Fast Times at Ridgemont High*	Vans Slip-on

Year	Name of movies	Sneakers
1982	*Blade Runner*	adidas Official
1982	*Tootsie*	Puma Suede
1980	*McVicar*	adidas TRX
1976	*All the President's Men*	adidas
1974	*Aliens*	Reebok Alien Stomper

Based on information sourced from a list compiled by Gary Warnett (http://www.complex.com/sneakers/2011/07/the-50-greatest-sneaker-moments-in-movies).

Sneakers as part of the growing streetwear industry

The streetwear industry which sneakers are a part of has been expanding its presence and market for the past decade. It is becoming a legitimate fashion genre with trade fairs and conventions. Streetwear refers to a distinct menswear style inspired by skate and surf culture as well as hip-hop culture, which is a type of fashion that the mainstream fashion took little notice of until quite recently. Steven Vogel explains what streetwear is all about:

> Streetwear is not about what you wear or how you wear it, but is a common set of ideals and experiences expressed visually and physically in the art and clothes that those who are part of the subculture produce. With streetwear, it's the feeling that counts. (Vogel 2007: 337)

Just like the bond that the sneaker enthusiasts create and exchange unspoken words, there is the spirit of streetwear culture. Vogel continues:

> Streetwear is at the core of an intensely independent urban subculture . . . . Not everything worn on the street is automatically streetwear, and neither is there a uniform code of clothing that makes streetwear what it is. Yet there is an unspoken understanding between those who wear streetwear and are involved in the subculture about what it is, or perhaps more specifically, what it is not. (Vogel 2007: 7)

The Magic Market, the biggest apparel tradeshow in the world that started in Las Vegas in 1933, organizes a number of tradeshows for streetwear. Agenda in New York is also another tradeshow that is rapidly expanding. Many of the streetwear companies that are run by young boys and men collaborate with sneaker companies to produce an exclusive pair:

> In order to distinguish itself as a major shoe brand and to get street credit with the skater and underground love for the rerelease, Nike got major skate companies like Zoo York, Supreme and London-based DJ Unkle to design patterns for the Dunk. The new breed formed the Nike SB Dunk, then offered only at skate shops and boutiques in limited quantities. Nike also took part in the popular X-Games that ESPN organized for the extreme sports fans. Since then, the SB Dunk has become a popular icon for enthusiastic sneaker collectors. (Lv and Huiguang 2007: 210)

Streetwear is basically casual, everyday wear for young boys which includes jeans, pants, T-shirts, sweat pants and shirts, bomber jackets, baseball caps, and sneakers, among others. It is not about the silhouette or the constructions of a garment that matters but the print designs and infographics[5] that would attract the streetwear followers. Along with sports and music, all of them are packaged as a specific lifestyle which draws male youths around the world. The streetwear industry is now a growing business which is becoming mainstream. Haenfler rightly questions:

> Subculturalists ... like to think of themselves as opposed to, separate from and superior to mainstream capitalist society, often including the business world. Yet subcultural life depends upon production and consumption, so where is the line between underground economics and mainstream co-optation? (Haenfler 2014: 139)

There is a contradiction between their wish to create something that is exclusive and hard to find and the desire to start a company to make into a lucrative business. Some subcultural members believe that the excessive commercialization of subcultures is unauthentic because they are supposed to be anti-mainstream and anti-dominant culture. The brands that emerged in the 1970s during the First Wave Sneaker Phenomenon were true to their underground subcultural philosophy and remained marginal. For instance, Zoo York was a clothing brand that came out of street culture in the late 1970s by a group of graffiti artists and skateboarders. No one knew or had to know its existence. Being marginal was precisely their selling point. Once a streetwear brand goes closer to the mainstream, it would be labeled as a "sell out."

Supreme, a retailer that started in 1994, is the best example of a streetwear brand that tries to stay true to their basic street culture ideology which is well described by Alex Williams, a *New York Times* reporter,

Passers-by in suits offered quizzical looks. But that's perfectly fine with Supreme. No offense, but if you don't know about Supreme, maybe it's because you're not supposed to. For much of its 18-year existence, Supreme was confined to the in-crowd, a scruffy clubhouse for a select crew of blunt-puffing skate urchins, graffiti artists, underground filmmakers and rappers....Huge lines, once endemic to its New York flagship in SoHo, now form at satellite stores in Los Angeles, London, Tokyo and other cities. The current issue of British GQ Style, a men's fashion bible, hails Supreme as "the coolest streetwear brand in the world right now." And the Berlin culture magazine *032c* called it "the Holy Grail of high youth street culture." The Business of Fashion site called it "the Chanel of downtown streetwear." (William 2012: E1)

The store was opened in New York by James Jebbia, and it caters mostly to skateboarders and sells streetwear to a small, segmented population of boys. But at the same time, it collaborates with well-known companies, such as Vans, Nike, and Comme des Garçons (Plates 4.16–4.18); the store never advertises its products as "limited editions" but sells only in small quantities. *Supreme* has become a model for anyone who wants to get into the streetwear business. Once again, "exclusivity" and "marginality" are very much celebrated and are the key components of their community.

Sneakers as postmodern fashion: Transcending categorical boundaries

Practicality and aesthetics are the two opposing functions, but sneaker enthusiasts show that they are indeed possible as readers can see in the images provided in this book. Fashion has never just been the property of the wealthy class. The desire for adornment and self-display is universal and found across cultures, classes, and races.

Bourdieu (1984) implies that the working class is not interested in adopting aesthetics, but this can be proved otherwise among sneaker enthusiasts. Even prior to the sneaker companies providing limited editions to satiate the appetite of the sneaker collectors, they would color and paint their sneakers to create something unique and aesthetic. It was important that they would stand out wearing special pairs when they play basketball in parks.

The diffusion of the sneaker popularity allowed the sneakers to become legitimate fashion. They have managed to transcend the boundary between practicality and adornment. Postmodernity is best characterized by the disappearance of cultural and social boundaries and categories. Postmodern elements can be found in a number of cultural phenomena, such as music, art, film, and fashion, and the conventional and normative standards are either challenged or put into question. Reilly and Cosbey give an example of postmodern fashion as follows:

> A designer might combine a soft, flowing "romantic" shirt with a pair of black leather pants and cowboy boots. Styles traditionally associated with different occasions or levels of formality, such as a tuxedo jacket and a pair of faded jeans, may be worn together. Formal fabrics, such as satin and velvet, may be used in casual dress; casual fabrics, such as denim and jersey knit, may be used in formal wear. Styles, patterns, or techniques associated with the dress or textiles from different parts of the world may be put together to form a multicultural look. (Reilly and Cosbey 2008: xv)

Postmodern ideas reject and negate any forms of categorizations and classifications as invalid since these groupings are fluid and socially constructed and can be destroyed any time. Whether a pair of sneakers matches casual wear or high fashion, or whether its functions are for adornment and sports, these questions even become insignificant in postmodernity. Sneakers are gradually transcending the class and race categories as they emerge from the underground to the more recognizable social surface. However, despite the postmodern message that the sneakers transmit to the world, there is one category that they stubbornly hang on to, and that is "male" because they need to make sure that their fashion practice is not female.

Conclusion

With the growing number of sneaker enthusiasts who pursue exclusive sneakers, boys and young men are treating self-display and fashion as a male affair while excluding girls and women from their community. The utilitarian and practical function of sneakers has shifted to the aesthetic function. Fashion and adornment that men had given up are now making a comeback. The commodification of the sneaker subculture with the help of the media has raised the popularity of sneakers that have become a fashion item. In today's postmodern age, categorical differences between male affair and a female affair is disappearing. The sneaker enthusiasts are not invading into the female domain, but rather, they are producing their own fashion domain as something uniquely masculine.

5

THE SNEAKER SUBCULTURE FROM DURKHEIMIAN PERSPECTIVES

Youth subcultural groups are often analyzed from a Marxist perspective as many of the researchers at the Center for Contemporary Cultural Studies (CCCS) have done. Their focus is on the concept of class and social differences that create inequalities. But, during my research on the sneaker subculture, the key concepts often found in subcultural studies, such as class, resistance, and deviance, did not appear to be all that salient, but instead it was gender, as I have indicated in the previous chapters. A Marxist interpretation of the sneaker subculture would be appropriate in discussing the First Wave Sneaker Phenomenon but not the current sneaker phenomenon. As I was conducting fieldwork on sneaker enthusiasts and their community, I could not help but think what Emile Durkheim (1858–1917) had written in the nineteenth century about social cohesion, a sense of belonging, anomie, and collective conscience among others in reference to modernity. Key concepts of a theory allow us to see part of social reality that we may not see otherwise. Studying concepts is the first step in analyzing and interpreting social phenomena, such as youth subcultures.

Durkheim was born and brought up in Lorraine, France, and after earning his degree at the École Normale Supérieure, he was invited to teach at the University of Bordeaux in 1887 where he started the first French sociology journal, *Année sociologique*. He wanted sociology to be a legitimate discipline because until then sociology was only part of economics and history. He is one of the most important sociologists who laid the foundation of sociological theories, structural-functionalism in particular, along with Karl Marx and Max Weber, and investigated society and social behavior in a macro-level analysis. Durkheim wanted to show how external social forces affected people's actions and decisions, and some of his major concerns about society were elements that held society together. I find this question to be relevant to today's growing youth subcultures that are strongly and loosely united and are starting to take shape not only in New York but also around the world. Durkheim's important books include *The Division of Labor* (1893), *Rules of the Sociological Method* (1895), *Suicide* (1897), and *The Elementary Forms of Religious Life* (1912).

In this chapter, I explain why and how Durkheim's various analytical concepts can be applied in the sociological analysis of the sneaker subculture that I have explained in this book. He made comparisons between the urban life and the rural life and studied the development of people's life into modern life. He was obviously talking about modernity and not postmodernity, but whatever he had said and described about modernity has been intensified, increased, and accelerated in postmodern society.

Connecting theory and practice

What is the purpose of explaining a subculture from a theoretical viewpoint, such as Durkheim's? There is no sociology without a theory. A social phenomenon without a theory would be a simple description of what goes on around us. As Mills (1959) argues, if theory is not connected to practical research, it remains abstract without any concrete evidence and is therefore meaningless. It has to be able to represent people's ways of living. Similarly, research also needs theory because, without a theory, research merely provides a series of facts that have happened, and one does not need to know sociology or be trained in sociology to tell factual stories.

Theory and research go hand in hand. Therefore, it is important to understand the meaning of a theory and the link between theory and practice. When we say "practice," we mean the practice of research that involves methodological inquiry. Facts and evidence are derived from practice. A theory does not seem to be connected to the real world or society in which we live in because of its abstractions and generalizations. But, in fact, our way of looking at the world depends on our theoretical perspectives. Structural functionalists, including Durkheim, often look at the functional aspects of people and society implying that everything has a purpose and a reason for existence; if not, it would slowly die out or disappear. On the other hand, if one takes a viewpoint of a conflict theory, which is an extension of Marxism, one would offer a critical perspective.

Therefore, theory and real life, such as a fashion phenomenon or a practice of sneaker collection, are very much tied together. To understand theory is to understand a great deal more about what and who we are and what the world is about. Practical issues embody certain theoretical assumptions, and by becoming more aware of them, we become more observant, analytical, and critical of social situations, whether it is about gender, class, race, or fashion issues.

Theories help us organize and reorganize our otherwise disorganized world, make sense of it, and guide us how we behave or should behave in it. They are created by developing a set of propositions or generalizations that establish relationships between things in some systematic way and are derived from information that people collect by seeing, hearing, touching, sensing, smelling, and feeling, which is the process of data collection. Therefore, the practice of research in this book was about the sneaker community which was made up of those who are passionate about sneakers while the major theoretical framework used to explain the sneaker phenomenon can be Durkheim's framework in addition to that of others, such as of Hebidge, Thornton, and Bourdieu.

Furthermore, besides Durkheim, the understanding of people's subjective meanings which is called Max Weber's interpretive sociology can also be used in subcultural studies and is also important in the sneaker studies as well. People do not simply behave but also engage in meaningful action, and it is the people that create these meanings. It is the interpretive sociologist's task not only to observe what people do but also to share the world of meaning and interpret why they behave the way they do. Therefore, buying and selling sneakers is not simply an action, but there is a deeper meaning behind the action which may not even be on the person's conscious mind. That is why it is sociologically significant to have a conversation with sneaker enthusiasts to hear about their love for and obsession with sneakers. One of them said to me, "My sneakers are more important than my girlfriend or my mom." While this is a humorous statement, sociologists would try to interpret what these words actually mean.

Transition from modernity to postmodernity

A modern society is often characterized by the advancement of technology, industrialization, individualism, and rationality, all of which mean that the modern society is firm, certain, and solid. People make rational and logical choices, and, therefore, their actions are always predictable. But the countries that are developed are entering into a new historical phase called postmodernity. No one can tell us exactly when modernity ended and when postmodernity started. There are still overlaps between the two while some characteristics are intensified in postmodernity, such as the globalization of economics, technological advancement, the blurring or the breakdown of inner and outer boundaries, and categories.

There are indications of cultural turmoil and upheaval everywhere. A broad social and cultural shift is taking place, and the concept of postmodernity by Crane (2000) and Muggleton (2000) captures some aspects of this transformation. The transition from modernity to postmodernity is a consequence of social, political, and cultural changes in the relationships between different social groups. Modernity presumes the existence of clear distinctions between different types and genres of aesthetic and stylistic expressions, while postmodernity no longer determines these categories as legitimate or meaningful. It is almost impossible to define what is legitimate or not legitimate, and this ideological as well as classificatory shift is relevant to the discussion of fashion.

As indicated earlier in the book, fashion emphasizes novelty and change that are the epitome of a postmodernist cultural form. Postmodernity is difficult to characterize because of its preoccupation with ambiguity and contradiction. Unlike modernity, it has no fixed or multiple meanings. Meanings are unstable, contradictory, and constantly changing. Subcultural identities that the youth create are fluid as well since their membership affiliation is flexible. They can jump from one subculture to the next if they wish.

Overcoming accelerated anomie in postmodern society

Modernity produces "anomie" which is a term coined by Durkheim and is central to understanding modernity, and its literal meaning is having no norms, and this is also an unintended consequence of modern urbanization and also globalization. Anomie is a state of having no regulations or a society with multiple norms which lead to one's inability to choose norms. I argue that Durkheim's concept of anomie has been further accelerated and strengthened as we transition into postmodern society. Human beings are essentially rule-following creatures since it gives structure to our life. A group of youths may reject and defy norms in a particular context, but they look for alternative norms that they appreciate and can follow, and that may lead and encourage some of them to form or be involved in a subculture which provides the members with different norms to follow, whether it is a way they tie their shoelaces or change the color every now and then, because that is an indication of one's allegiance and membership to the group. Subculture consists of a natural formation of rules that are made by the insider members, and these rules bind people together.

Phillippe Bernard, in his article "The True Nature of Anomie" (1988: 93), defined anomie as "one characterized by indeterminate goals and unlimited aspirations, the disorientation or vertigo created by confrontation with an excessive widening of the horizons of the possible." While modernity offers multiple opportunities and possibilities, people are confused by these choices that they are confronted with, and it may even result in social confusion and chaos. Haenfler also writes about the unpredictability and the instability of postmodernity (2014: 118): "Postmodern identity is temporary, unstable, and fluid."

One's subcultural affiliation tells the members, what to do, what to follow, how to behave, and so on. Being a "true sneakerhead" requires them to follow the latest trends and get hold of limited editions sneakers, make sure their sneakers are always clean and almost brand new, find out what the latest shoelaces look like, where the next sneaker convention will take place, which pairs to buy or sell at what price, and so on.

Social cohesion, collective conscience, and mechanical/organic solidarity

A state of anomie reduces the level of social cohesion since being unable to decide which path to take means not knowing where or which group to belong. For Durkheim, too little (or excessive) social integration or cohesion was detrimental to people and society.

One of Durkheim's greatest concerns was social integration, solidarity, and cohesion, that is, to what extent people were connected to each other and what holds society together. It is not an easy task to measure the level of social cohesion in quantifiable numbers, but Durkheim had made an attempt to do so in his widely read sociology book *Suicide* (1897) by analyzing suicide rates. He explains the reasons why people voluntarily kill themselves based on the lower and higher suicide rates which are related to the depth and the degree of social cohesion which also affects one's well-being.

Furthermore, in his *Division of Labor* (1893), Durkheim talked about mechanical solidarity and organic solidarity which exist in traditional society and modern society, respectively. He mainly talked about them in reference to religion. He explained that the growing population density undermined mechanical solidarity whereby societies are held together because individual differences are minimized, and people have common beliefs and similar occupations. People used to be more or less self-sufficient in preindustrial stage such as food collection, production, and consumption. Durkheim also pointed out that totemic religion plays an important role in bringing people together and creating a common "collective consciousness" that they can share with each other in traditional and homogenous societies where there is mechanical solidarity. Traditions, rituals, and regular practices also bring collective conscience making an object as a totemic symbol.

Over time, mechanical solidarity is replaced by organic solidarity of more advanced societies which are held together by the interdependence that results from a highly complex division of labor. But, in a modern urban environment, we have specialized tasks, and therefore, we are not self-sufficient and need to be connected with each other. Durkheim explains that it is the division of labor that gives a foundation of solidarity among modern people. As a society becomes increasingly modernized, people's division of labor is accelerated. There are multiple layers and ranks in labor which means that people must rely on each other and cooperate with each other for survival since one person cannot do everything by himself or herself. This phenomenon requires interdependence which brings people together physically and morally. In addition, people's tasks become more individualized.

While sneakers are not a sacred object (although they may be from the collectors' perspective), it is a symbolic object that brings the subcultural members together emotionally and physically. Sneaker enthusiasts treat sneakers as something similar to a totemic symbol that binds them with fellow sneaker fans which in turn brings about "collective conscience" which Durkheim defines as follows (1893: 105): "The totality of beliefs and sentiments common to the average members of a society forms a determinate system with a life of its own. It can be termed the collective or creative consciousness."

There is a gradual loss and lack of overall, macro-scale collective conscience in postmodern society, so the youths look for it elsewhere. Human beings must share collective conscience with someone as long as they remain social. As the postmodern society becomes global, pluralist, and diverse, which can all be positive, they also generate a great deal of "anomie." Whenever there are multiple norms, we get lost and cannot choose which norms to follow, which is equivalent to having no norms at all. According to Durkheim, laws and customs are the basis of collective conscience which are social and come from common beliefs and norms that are carried over from generation to generation, and it is "the totality of beliefs and sentiments common to the average citizens of the society" (Durkheim 1893: 79).

Through repeated interactions and communications, the members of the sneaker subculture construct certain degrees of subcultural solidarity which is more mechanical than organic. Their emotional involvement in and attachment to the group gets deeper and deeper as their passion for sneakers gets more intense. As Randall Collins writes (1981: 985): "patterned interactions generate the central features of social organization—authority … and group membership— by creating and recreating 'mythical' cultural symbols and emotional energies." And they come from the feeling of collectivity based on their subcultural membership.

Using Durkheim's framework, Collins also argues that when people are in the physical presence of others, there is a higher degree of mutual surveillance. The more people feel they are accepted by the group, the more they conform to the group's norms; conversely, the less they are around others, the more their attitudes are explicitly individualistic and self-centered (Collins 1981). Staying together in the same physical space increases stronger and higher level of emotional attachment, which is a natural outcome of mobilization.

However, as we move into the postmodern age, geographical locations of a subculture is no longer significant for the members as they communicate via social media. During the Second and Third Wave Sneaker Phenomenon, the sneaker enthusiasts were connected through "virtual collective conscience" using the Internet and the social media. The belief that they are connected and bonded based on their virtual communication was sufficient enough for them to identify themselves as a subcultural member. There were psychological satisfaction and instant gratification in confirming their bond through online social interaction. One of the sneaker collectors said to me:

> I have never met seventy percent of the people that I talk to every day through twitter and Instagram. I don't even know what they look like, their race, or what they do for living, or whether they are employed or unemployed. I don't even know their real names. I don't know where they live unless we are trading sneakers. But one thing we know is that we are all crazy about sneakers.

Sneaker enthusiasts move back and forth between personal and impersonal space. Their love for sneakers unites them on a personal and emotional level, but at the same time, they guard their private, physical space.

Conclusion

I have applied Durkheim's theoretical perspectives in analyzing the sneaker subculture using his famous concepts, such as anomie, collective conscience, and social cohesion among others. Whether Durkheimian perspectives would apply to other youth subcultures or not is debatable, and that is for me and other researchers to further investigate the question. Just as no object is too mundane for a sociological analysis, no social and collective phenomenon is too trivial to study as a sociological topic. At the same time, I confirm and reconfirm to myself the greatness of Emile Durkheim as a social theorist and the grand social theory he has left behind.

CONCLUSION: FUTURE DIRECTIONS AND POSSIBILITIES IN FOOTWEAR STUDIES

I have shown in this book that a research focus on sneakers can be part of fashion and dress studies including footwear. It could also be placed within gender studies and subcultural studies. My research on sneakers is not complete. Nor did I answer all the questions I had at the start of my research. In fact, I have more questions now. One of my former advisors in graduate school and a prominent sociologist, Harrison White, once said to me: "An item, an object or a phenomenon can be analyzed and explored from a million perspectives. Scholars can always collaborate to produce better research." I always keep his words in my heart as I finish writing my book to remind myself that it is not the end of this research. In this conclusion chapter, I offer some themes and perspectives that scholars, including myself and other sociologists in particular, can possibly investigate as an extension of footwear studies or a continuation of my research on sneakers.

My research was focused mainly from the consumers' side rather than the producers' or the manufacturers' side since they are the participants that form a subculture which is often studied from the members' perspectives, and scholars make an attempt to investigate their distinct values, norms, beliefs, and attitudes. But as indicated in my research as well as others, subcultures are commodified and commercialized so that their subcultural objects are manufactured in the industries, and thus, we need to look at the producers' side of subcultures. For the sneakers, the gatekeeping function of the sneaker trend and fashion can be elaborated and researched further to understand who exactly is controlling and manipulating exclusive sneakers. One could even further explore the gender component of sneaker enthusiasts and study the role of female sneaker collectors, if there are any, in comparison to female members in other subcultures. There may even be the Fourth Wave Sneaker Phenomenon, or we may already be entering into that phase.

Most of my empirical work was conducted in New York, but many had told me that there are rare sneakers found only in Japan, and it is a goldmine for western sneaker enthusiasts. I met an Australian sneaker dealer in Japan who told me:

> I initially came to Japan as a teacher. I wanted to be here because there are great sneakers in Japan. Then friends back home started asking me to buy some pairs that are found only in Japan. I started getting so many orders, and I became so busy that I had to quit my teaching job. I now buy and sell sneakers full-time in Tokyo.

Sneakers enthusiasts in Japan still form a small community, although they are very much updated with the latest sneakers in the United States and Europe. There are no conventions or events that are similar to the ones found overseas. A comparative analysis of different sneaker subcultures around the world could be a potential focus for next research.

The expansion and growth of subcultures inform us the youths' need to participate in a structured group. As our society becomes increasingly globalized, diverse, and technologically advanced, which requires less face-to-face communication, people look for places to belong because that will in turn affect their well-being. Understanding the youths will help us address their as well as societal issues and problems as they are a reflection of what is happening in the world. A story about sneaker enthusiasts is an example of a community that is bound together by common interests, values, and beliefs. Human beings are more likely to associate with those who are similar to themselves, and that becomes increasingly difficult in a diverse world. By exploring other youth subcultures from a global perspective, we can place them in a marcostructural perspective to understand the world.

The value transition of sneakers from a mundane object into a fashion item shows that the value of a physical object is socially constructed. High or low values attached to an object are not inherent in the object itself, but we as a society create the values and the meanings. Sneakers are also an epitome of what fashion is since they consist of major factors of what fashion is, such as an emphasis on novelty and exclusivity. Although some sneakers have been elevated to "fashion" in terms of price points and social status, sneakers still are devalued in some social contexts. Joe Palazzolo writes in the Wall Street Journal Law blog about how a juror should dress in the courtroom:

> In the Orlando division of the US District Court for the Middle District of Florida, the dress code goes like this: You are expected to conduct yourself with reserve and courtesy, and when appearing at the courthouse, must dress appropriately to preserve the dignity of the Court. Proper attire includes coat

and tie for men and similarly appropriate attire for women. No jeans, polo shirts or sneakers. (Palazzolo 2014)

This story indicates the persistent devaluation of sneakers, or any flat shoes without heels, as low-status footwear. In addition, the 2015 Cannes Film Festival became the center of controversy and the world's attention when it was reported by the media that several women in their fifties were turned away from a red carpet screening at the festival because they were wearing Rhinestone-encrusted flats instead of heels (BBC News 2015). Although it was never officially confirmed by the festival, it appeared that heels were part of their unwritten dress code for women. What makes a pair of shoes appropriate or inappropriate for an occasion or an event? Is it just about the height of a heel? The relationship between footwear and its social status in contemporary society continues to be an intriguing topic.

Furthermore, studies on shoes and footwear can extend to the study on feet. It is not only women's high heels that have erotic connotations but also their barefeet, ankles, and small feet. Transko writes:

So strong was the sexual symbolism of the foot that in seventeenth-century Spain when Queen Maria Luisa of Savoy, the wife of Philip V, fell off her horse and was dragged around the palace courtyard with her foot caught in the stirrup, several lords just looked on in horror—to help would mean touching her foot, a fiercely taboo act. The man who finally saved her had to take refuge in a monastery until he received a royal pardon for his act. (Trasko 1989: 12)

Similarly, in her historical study of Japanese footwear (2011), Chaikin explains that footwear was unclean both from its contact with the ground and the feet, and therefore, leaving the feet exposed was an expression of intimacy in early modern Japan. Feet, symbolic of the genitals, have a definite erotic focus. In art, curled toes indicated arousal, and the feet of women who were not prostitutes or of low social status were rarely shown. Imagery for men was quite different; barefoot men were often meant to represent marital estrangement, and piles of shoes meant probably the infidelity of one's husband (Chaikin 2011: 175). As for the Indian culture, the foot is one of the most admired parts of the female body in the Indian perception of romanticism and eroticism. This may be one of the reasons why young girls and women decorate the soles of their feet in very special ways, for example, by coloring them with red kumkum paste, by using these to paint intricate designs on, or by tattooing the foot (Jain-Neubauer 2000: 20). Philippe Perrot also explains the erotic implication of an ankle: "In the nineteenth century, female bosoms and behinds were emphasized, but legs were completely hidden, distilling into the lacy foam of underwear an erotic capital, the returns on which could be gauged by the cult of the calf and by the arousal caused by the glimpse of an ankle" (Perrot 1996: 105). Wearing high heels was a way to construct femininity and be the object of male gaze and sexual desire.

In addition to barefeet, the size of a woman's foot was also a symbol of femininity and female virtue. In the western world, small feet were also regarded as aristocratic, a most exquisite expression of femininity (Transko 1989).

We see the value of a small female foot in the famous Cinderella story written in the late seventeenth century. Cinderella's small feet and glass slippers symbolized her inborn beauty, grace, nobility, and femininity. There are similar versions of the story throughout the world. There is the Chinese version that is very similar to Cinderella in which all the main elements of the plot are included, such as the jealous stepmother, the animal medium, the grand ball, and the lost shoe (Ko 2001: 25).

While Cinderella is a fictional character, the practice of keeping girls' feet as tiny as possible known as footbinding is a historical fact.[1] This practice is unique to and localized in Chinese culture. It is known as The Chinese Lily Foot, which is believed to have begun at the end of the eleventh century in China after the fall of the Tang Dynasty and lasted into the 1930s in spite of having been outlawed. A young girl's foot was wrapped with a cloth as tightly as possible, bending the small toes backwards under the sole of the foot, which is an extremely painful and torturous practice. After a while, the nerves and muscles are destroyed. The cloth is unwrapped every now and then to wash the feet, but they remain wrapped making sure the feet does not grow and remains tiny.

According to Dorothy Ko (2001:15), while the practice of footbinding which originated in the Confucian culture has been oversimplified by western scholars as "women being the victims of beauty" or "men fetishized tiny feet," this is not entirely wrong, although there are more complex and nuanced meanings behind this practice. It is undeniable that men were attracted to small feet and found them exotic and erotic, and footbinding was born of a male fantasy that turned women into sexual objects.

> Footbinding was entirely reasonable course of action for a woman who lived in a Confucian culture that placed the highest moral value on domesticity, motherhood, and handwork. The ideal Confucian woman was who worked diligently with her hands and body, and those who did so were amply rewarded in terms of power in the family, communal respect, and even imperial recognition. The binding of feet created a woman who fit these ideals. (Ko 2001: 15)

Such ideals and values confining women's mobility and social activities within the domestic territory are patriarchal in nature. The tiny feet and tiny shoes were erotically appealing to men. Beverley Jackson also explores the mysterious and erotic quality of the feet encased inside tiny shoes as follows:

Very rarely would a Chinese man ever see a bound foot without the white bandages covering it. He might know what every other part of the woman's body looked like, including the genitals. Her body was very real to him, but the feet were literally shrouded in mystery. In his mind, they could be as beautiful and desirable as he wished them to be. Those mysterious bound feet offered countless opportunities for dreaming and fantasizing. (Jackson 1997: 107)

Bound feet figured heavily in sex with prostitutes. Certainly, no successful prostitute ever had big feet. Because their feet were such an important part of their profession, high-class prostitutes and courtesans often went to extremes to create exceedingly small feet and exceptionally beautiful shoes. A man going into a house of prostitution would not be looking for a pretty face or large breasts. He chose his prospective partner by judging the size of her feet from the size of her shoes (Jackson 1997: 111).

Whether it is high heels or bound small feet, it confines women in a specific space and restricts them from moving around freely. These are the ways in which shoes were used to control women's mobility. However, immobility was indicative of an aristocratic standard and was, therefore, a status symbol. The less a woman walked, the higher her social prominence. In sixteenth-century Venice, extremely high platforms became fashionable, and they were so high that women needed someone to support them in order to walk (Vianello 2011). A woman's physical immobility is a reflection of her social immobility. The changes in footwear designs represent women's diverse social roles.

According to Judith Miller (2009), who makes a convincing correlation between women's social roles and the type of footwear that they wore, in the early nineteenth century, flat pumps echoed a desire for equality following American Independence and the French Revolution. As the century progressed, decorated, heeled shoes were the ideal for hooped crinoline skirts, while dainty boots modestly hid a lady's ankles. In the early nineteenth century, high heels had been replaced by flat shoes. But, by the late nineteenth century, they came back again, and in the early twentieth century, new freedoms meant women wore boots suitable for a more active lifestyle (Miller 2009:17). This is a topic worth pursuing further to understand how the hegemonic ideal about femininity is perpetuated through footwear and feet.

Furthermore, research on feet can extend to feet decorations, pedicure, or jewelries that accessorize ankles and toes. In addition, footwear almost always is worn with legwear, such as stockings or tights. Scholars have yet to study the history of legwear in the West and the non-West. Like high heels, stockings used to be worn by both men and women, but it has now become a female object.

Studies on historical and contemporary footwear can also lead to further research on shoemakers and shoe designers. They also deserve more scholarly attention as its occupational status has been elevated since modernity. We can see a correlation between a social class and those who are involved in the shoemaking process. Many scholars write that historically the social position of a shoemaker or a cobbler had been at the bottom of the social structure both in western and non-western countries. Shoemakers were not designers.

According to Chaiklin (2011), footwear makers were considered an outcaste class in early modern Japan, since they dealt with leather that came from dead animals, such as cows, wild boars, deer, and monkeys. Not all footwear were made from leather, but the idea of uncleanliness was extended to encompass the entire category, and monopolies with strict, guild-like practices resulted in the designation of all shoemakers as an outcaste class (Chaiklin 2011: 173). A Dutch merchant who was living in Nagasaki, Japan, in the late 1820s writes:

> In the Japanese social hierarchy, the absolute lower of all the craftsman was the leather tanner.... These unfortunate men who practice this profession, in the fullest sense of the worlds, are cast out of society. They always live in an isolated and remote street, and everyone who is not of their profession despises them, avoiding as much familiarity as possible. (quoted in Chaiklin 2011: 172–173)

Similarly, in ancient India, leather workers of any description, be they tanners or shoemakers, always occupied one of the lowest positions in Indian caste system and were considered untouchables as, like early modern Japan, leather and all products made of dead animals were considered impure and contaminating in the Indian cultural context. Therefore, touching leather or leather objects was prohibited to purists. Even accidental contact with an untouchable by a member of the higher caste was considered a source of great pollution and required ritual ablutions (Jain-Neubauer 2000: 112).

The lower social status of a shoemaker is also found in the western footwear makers. The London bootmaker, James Dacres Devlin, wrote about the meager salaries of shoemakers in London and the deterioration of their professional and personal standards of living in the transition of shoemaking from "gentle craft" to "sweater trade" (quoted in McNeil and Riello 2011b: 17).

There was social distinction between a shoemaker and a cobbler whose social status was even lower than that of the shoemaker. Walford points out:

> Shoemaking developed into a profession in ancient Rome when artisans congregated near city market places.... Like many craftsmen, shoemakers created guilds from the twelfth century, which acted as professional associations, unions and regulatory boards, protecting shoemakers, their suppliers and their clients from unfair business practices and pricing while

ensuring quality products. Shoemakers learned their trade over a period of years through unpaid apprenticeship to master shoemakers. They were licensed by guilds only once they had mastered the skills of construction and finishing .... Guilds were not open to cobblers, who were shoe repairers. Shoemakers were capable of doing repairs but it was considered beneath their abilities. (Walford 2007: 12)

But the system of apprenticeship created masters of shoemakers who had learnt everything about manufacturing techniques. They made changes in construction techniques and fabrics, or the curve of a heel. However, modernity has transformed the social meaning of shoemaking into shoe designing. Shoemakers are now shoe designers who enjoy and share a glamorous status with a fashion designer.

The shoe designer did not always have the status in the fashion world that he has achieved today. The first shoemaker to achieve any fame at all was Yanturni, about whom nothing is known except that he was of Asian extraction and was the curator at the Cluny Museum in the early years of this century. (McDowell 1989: 7)

Pietro Yantorny (1874–1936) was an Italian shoemaker with a prominent socialite as his clientele. Morales (2013: 7) also writes: "In the past, making or repairing shoes was considered a humble trade, comparable to that of carpenters, blacksmiths or seamstresses. However, the relentless pace of today's footwear industry means that a handcrafted shoe has become a prized item created by highly skilled professionals."

Many of the well-known contemporary shoe designers were once shoemakers and cobblers. For instance, Salavatore Ferragamao (1898–1960) opened his store in Hollywood for shoe repair and custom-made shoes. Ferragamo is known as one of the most famous luxury footwear brands. Jimmy Choo was born into a family of shoemakers in Malaysia, and it was his father who taught him how to make shoes. He was discovered by and partnered with an editor at British Vogue who made his shoes well known to celebrities. He sold his company in 2001, but the brand name Jimmy Choo represents an elegant and decorative shoe. The social status of a shoemaker has been elevated to the level of an artist or a creator.[2]

Therefore, research on sneakers offers more possibilities and directions in footwear studies and fashion and dress studies. There are multiple areas, topics, and approaches to this field. I welcome other fashion scholars and researchers in social sciences to develop further academic research on shoes, feet, shoemakers, and subcultures, using my work as a departing point for sociological debates and discussions.

NOTES

Introduction

1   Bobbito Garcia is a writer and a DJ, known as the father of a sneaker subculture and the author of a book *Where'd You Get Those? New York City's Sneaker Culture: 1960–1987* (2003); Ronnie Fieg is a designer and owner of Kith, a sneaker boutique in Manhattan and Brooklyn. He is known for his Gel Lyte III, which he collaborated on with Asics; Jeff Staple is an owner of Reed Space in Manhattan and Staple Design, a design agency. One of his trademark sneakers is Nike Pigeon Dunk that was released in 2005, and it was so popular that it almost caused a riot at his store; Jeff Harris is a sneaker connoisseur and one of the founders of Roc'n Sole, a sneaker boutique in Brooklyn, along with Lenny Santiago, and Tyran "Ty Ty" Smith; Eugene Kan is former Managing Director of Hypebeast.com, a globally popular streetwear website based in Hong Kong; Pete Forester is a writer for Complex Magazine who used to work for Ronnie Fieg; and Yuming Wu is a founder of Sneakernews.com, a sneaker website, and the SneakerCon, a sneaker convention that takes place in different cities in the United States and allows sneaker enthusiasts to trade their shoes on the spot.

2   I only had two pairs of sneakers when I started my research on sneakers, but by the time I finished writing this book, I had twenty pairs. As my research progressed, I began to understand the appeal of sneakers which have two opposing functions: comfort and beauty. But at the same time, I found out that the selection of female sneakers is limited, especially for women like myself who have small feet, such as size 5.

3   http://www.statisticbrain.com/footwear-industry-statistics/

4   For the historical development of each sneaker company, see *The Sneaker Book: Anatomy of an Industry and an Icon* (1998) by Tom Vanderbilt; *Trainers: Over 300 Classics from Rare Vintage to the Latest Designs* (2003) by Neal Heard; *Sneakers* (2007) by Luo Lv and Zhang Huiguang; "The Origins of the Modern Shoes, 1945–1975" (unpublished PhD dissertation) by Thomas Turner.

Chapter 1

1   June Swann has published two other books on European footwear: *Shoes* (1982) and *Shoemaking* (1986). For other studies on European historical footwear, see "Part I: A Foot in the Past" in *Shoes: A History from Sandals to Sneakers* (2011: 2–159) edited by Peter McNeil and Giorgio Riello.

2   Valerie Steele writes extensively on fashion, high heels, and eroticism: See *Fashion and Eroticism* (1985), *The Corset: A Cultural History* (2001), *Shoes: A Lexicon of Style* (1999). For others, also see Elizabeth Semmelhack's article "A Delicate Balance: Women, Power and High Heels," in *Shoes: A History from Sandals to Sneakers* (2011: 224–249); Lisa Small's *Killer Heels: The Art of the High-Heeled Shoe Exhibition Catalogue* (2014); Ivan Vartanin's article "Introduction: Nude In Heels, or a Fetish for Photography" in *High Heels: Fashion, Femininity, Seduction* (2011: 12–35); Caroline Weber, Caroline's "The Eternal High Heel: Eroticism and Empowerment" in *the Killer Heels: The Art of the High-Heeled Shoe Exhibition Catalogue* (2014).

Chapter 2

1   See "American Traditions I" and "American Traditions II" in *Subcultural Theory: Traditions and Concepts* (2011) by J. Patrick William; "Part I: The Chicago School of Urban Ethnography" in *The Subcultures Readers* edited by Ken Gelder.

2   See "British Traditions I" and "British Traditions II" in *Subcultural Theory: Traditions and Concepts* (2011) by J. Patrick William. "Part II: The Birmingham Tradition and Cultural Studies" in *The Subcultures Readers* edited by Ken Gelder.

3   The traditional feminist thinking begins with Mary Wollstonecraft's *A Vindication of the Rights of Women* (1792) and John Stuart Mill's *The Subjugation of Women* (1869). But feminism as an organized movement began as the first-wave feminism took place in Europe and the United States in the late nineteenth and the early twentieth centuries. The second wave refers to the period between 1960s and 1970s which took place within the context of civil rights and antiwar movement. The third wave begins in the 1980s and 1990s. Some are now even talking about the fourth wave. See more in *In Their Time: A History of Feminism in Western Society* (2001) by Marlene Legates.

4   The earliest use of the term "subculture" in sociology seems to be its application as a subdivision of a national culture by Alfred McLung Lee in 1945 and Milton M. Gordon in 1947 (Brake 1980: 5); they stressed the significance of socialization within the cultural subsections of a pluralist society. Chris Jenks (2004: 7) says that definitions and versions proliferate, and origins are obscure, and it has been argued by Marvin E. Wolfgang and Franco Ferracuti in 1967 that the term subculture is not widely used in the social sciences literature until after the Second World War. Phil Cohen (1972) defined subculture as a compromise solution between two contradictory needs: the need to create and express autonomy and difference from parents and the need to maintain the parental identification.

5   For Michael Jordan's life and accomplishments, see *Michael Jordan: The Life* (2014) by Roland Lazenby; *There Is No Next: NBA Legends on the Legacy of Michael Jordan* (2014) by Sam Smith.

6   Davidson also refers to other literary works by Andersen, such as *The Little Mermaid* (1836), *The Girl Who Trod on a Loaf* (1859), and *The Snow Queen* (1844), in which he makes literary allusions of the red shoes.

7   See http://www.complex.com/sneakers/2013/07/greatest-sneaker-controversies ("The 25 Most Controversial Things that Ever Happened in Sneakers" by Russ Bengtson).

Chapter 3

1   In Japanese subcultures, it is girls who play a major role. They spend a great deal of resources on clothes and makeup. Fashion is of utmost importance because they want to stand out and be noticed; some may wish to rebel against the formal and traditional ways. They generally hang out in large groups around train stations and chat. The girl teens who belong to the street subcultures are sometimes treated as deviant by the rest of Japanese society, but they are bound by their strength in numbers and are always with friends who dress in a similar style. Instead of finding a place within the male-dominant subcultures, these Japanese girls created and maintain their own autonomy and independence despite their expression of excessive cuteness and femininity (see Kawamura 2012).

2   Margaret Mead's research in 1935 was one of the first studies to question the relationship between sex and gender which are often treated as interchangeable terms since the public as well as scholars had assumed that one's biological trait would automatically guide gender. Mead proved this assumption false through her research on three tribal groups in New Guinea.

Chapter 4

1   The first book that was written about Beau Brummel was by Captain Jesse called *The Life of George Brummel, Esq., Commonly Called Beau Brummel* (1844) in two volumes. In 1924, Eleanor Parker bought an old manuscript "Male and Female Costume" in New York which was listed as an original, unpublished manuscript by Brummell bound in two volumes and dated 1822. It was published in 1932 as a book entitled *Male and Female Costume: Grecian and Roman Costume British Costume from the Roman Invasion until 1822 and the Principles of Costume Applied to the Improved Dress of the Present Day*. On Dandy, see *Gender on the Divide: The Dandy in Modernist Literature* (1993) by Jessica R. Feldman; *Dandyism and Transcultural Modernity: The Dandy, the Flaneur, and the Translator in 1930s Shanghai, Tokyo and Paris* (2010) by Hsiao-yen Peng; *The Ultimate Man of Style* (2006) by Ian Kelly; *The Dandy* (1960) by Eleanor Moers. For social aspects of dandym, see Domna Stanton's *The Aristocrat as Art: A Study of Honnête Homme and the Dandy in Seventeenth- and Nineteenth-Century French Literature* (1980).

2   Riello and McNeil write, "an unexpected parallelism can be demonstrated in late eighteenth century Europe, where the bleaching boots was part of the ritual of a gentleman's behavior" (Riello and McNeil 2011b: 5).

3   See *Fashion-ology: An Introduction to Fashion Studies* (2005) by Yuniya Kawamura.

4   See http://www.complex.com/sneakers/2013/01/the-50-greatest-sneaker-references-in-rap-history (Brian Josephs, "The 50 Best Sneaker References in Rap History" by Brian Josephs).

5   Infographics are graphic visual representations of information, data, or knowledge intended to present complex information (Wikipedia.com).

Conclusion

1   For footbinding, see also *Cinderella's Sisters: A Revisionist History of Footbinding* (2007) by Dorothy Ko; *Aching for Beauty: Footbinding in China* (2002) by Wang Ping.

2   For contemporary shoe designers' works, see *Shoes: A Celebration of Pumps, Sandals, Slippers and More* (1996) by Linda O'Keefe; *Shoes A-Z: Designers, Brands, Manufactures and Retailers* (2010) by Jonathan Walford; *Footwear Design* (2012) by Aki Choklat.

BIBLIOGRAPHY

Adams, Nathaniel (2013), *I Am Dandy: The Return of the Elegant Gentleman*, with Rose Callahan, photographer, Berlin, Germany: Gestalten.

Adshead, Samuel Adrian Miles (1997), *Material Culture in Europe and China, 1400–1800*, Basingstoke: Macmillan.

Aheran, Charlie (2003), "The Gangs of New York City, Hip-Hop & Sneakers" in *The Trainers: Over 300 Classics from Rare Vintage to the Latest Designs*, edited by Neal Heard, London: Carlton Books, pp. 20–23.

Akinwumi, Tunde M. (2011), "Interrogating Africa's Past: Footwear Among the Yoruba" in *Shoes: A History from Sandals to Sneakers*, edited by Peter McNeil and Giorgio Riello, Paperback Edition, London: Berg, pp. 182–195.

Alexander, Jeffrey (ed.) (1988), *Durkheimian Sociology*, Cambridge: Cambridge University Press.

Althusser, Louis (1988), "Ideology and Ideological State Apparatuses" in *Cultural Theory and Popular Culture: A Reader*, edited by John Storey, London: Prentice Hall, pp. 153–164.

Anderson, Mark and Mark Jenkins (2001), *Dance of Days*, New York: Soft Skull Press.

Anderson, Nels (1922), *The Hobo*, Chicago, IL: University of Chicago Press.

Appadurai, Arjun (1990), "Disjuncture and Difference in the Global Cultural Economy", *Theory, Culture, and Society* 7: 295–310.

Arnold, David O. (1970), *The Sociology of Subcultures*, Berkeley, CA: The Glendessary Press.

Aspers, Patrik (2005), *Markets in Fashion: A Phenomenological Approach*, London: Routledge.

Baizerman, Suzanne, Joanne B. Eicher and Catherine Cerny (2008), "Eurocentrism in the Study of Ethnic Dress" in *The Visible Self: Global Perspectives on Dress, Culture, and Society*, edited by Joanne B. Either, Sandra Lee Evenson and Hazel A. Lutz, New York: Fairchild Publications, Inc., pp. 123–132.

Banner, Lois (2008), "The Fashionable Sex, 1100–1600" in *Men's Fashion Reader*, edited by Andrew Reilly and Sarah Cosbey, New York: Fairchild Books, pp. 6–16.

Barker, Chris (2004), *Sage Dictionary of Cultural Studies*, London: Sage.

Barnard, Malcolm (1998), *Art, Design and Visual Culture*, New York: Palgrave Macmillan.

Barnard, Malcolm (2001), *Approaches to Understanding Visual Culture*, New York: Palgrave Macmillan.

Barnard, Malcolm (2007), *Fashion Theory: A Reader*, London: Routledge.

Barnard, Malcolm (2008), *Fashion as Communication*, London: Routledge.

Baron, Stephen (1989), "Resistance and Its Consequences: The Street Culture of Punks", *Youth Society*, 21, 2: 207–237.

Barthes, Roland (1964), *Elements of Semiology*, translated by A. Lavers and C. Smith, New York: Hill and Wang.

Barthes, Roland (1967), *The Fashion System*, translated by M. Ward and R. Howard, New York: Hill and Wang.

Barthes, Roland (1977), *Image, Music, Text*, translated by S. Heath, London: Montana.

BBC News (2015), "Cannes Film Festival 'Turns Away Women in Flat Shoes'", *Entertainment and Arts*, May 19. (bbc.com/news/entertainment-arts)

Beauvoir, Simone de (1949), *The Second Sex*, translated by H. M. Parshley, New York: Penguin.

Becker, Howard ([1963] 1973), *Outsiders*, Glencoe, NY: Free Press.

Becker, Howard (1982), *Art World*, Berkeley, CA: University of California Press.

Beer, Robert (2004), *Tibetan Ting Sha*, London: Connections Press.

Bell, Daniel (1973), *The Coming of Post-Industrial Society*, New York: Basic Books.

Bell, Daniel (1976), *The Cultural Conditions of Capitalism*, New York: Basic Books.

Bell, Quentin ([1947] 1976), *On Human Finery*, London: Hogarth Press.

Bengtson, Russ (2013), "Digging and Deadstock: Sneaker Collecting Then and Now" in *SLAM KICKS*, edited by Ben Osborne, New York: Universe Publishing, pp. 87–90.

Bennett, Andy (2000), *Popular Music and Youth Culture: Music, Identity and Place*, London: Macmillan.

Bennett, Andy (2005), *Culture and Everyday Life*, London: Sage.

Bennett, Andy (2006), "Punk's Not Dead: The Continuing Significance of Punk Rock for an Older Generation of Fans", *Sociology*, 40, 2: 219–235.

Bennett, Andy and Keith Kahn-Harris (2004), *After Subculture: Critical Studies in Contemporary Youth Culture*, London: Palgrave Macmillan.

Bennett, Andy and Paul Hodkinson (eds.) (2012), *Ageing and Youth Cultures: Music, Style and Identity*, London: Berg.

Bennett, Andy and Richard A. Peterson (2004), *Music Scenes: Local, Translocal, and Virtual*, Nashville, TN: Vanderbilt University Press.

Bennett, Tony, Michael Emmison and John Frow (1999), *Accounting for Taste*, Melbourne, Australia: Cambridge University Press.

Bernard, Phillippe (1988), "The True Nature of Anomie", *Sociological Theory*, 6: 91–95, New York: Sage Publications.

Bibort, Alan (2009), *Beatniks: A Guide to an American Subculture*, Westport, CT: Greenwood.

Blake, Mark (ed.) (2008), *Punk-The Whole Story*, New York: DK.

Blanco, José F. (2011), "The Postmodern Age: 1960-2010" in *The Fashion Reader*, edited by Linda Welters and Abby Lillethun, Oxford: Berg.

Bleikhorn, Samantha (2002), *The Mini-Mod Sixties Book*, San Francisco, CA: Last Gasp.

Blum, Sasha (2009), *The Gothic Subculture: An Empirical Investigation of the Psychological and Behavioral Characteristics of Its Affiliates*, Saarbrücken, Germany: VDM Verlag.

Blumenthal, Erica M. (2015), "Updated: Snow Tires for the Feet", *The New York Times*, February 12, p. E3.

Blumer, Herbert (1969), "Fashion: From Class Differentiation to Collective Selection", *The Sociological Quarterly*, 10, 3: 275–291.

Blümlein, Jürgen, Daniel Schmid and Dirk Vogel (2008), *Made for Skate: The Illustrated History of Skateboard Footwear*, Berlin, Germany: Gingko Press.

Blundell, Sue (2011), "Beneath Their Shining Feet: Shoes and Sandals in Classical Greece" in *Shoes: A History from Sandals to Sneakers*, edited by Peter McNeil and Giorgio Riello, Paperback Edition, Oxford: Berg, pp. 30–49.

Blush, Steven (2001), *American Hardcore, A Tribal History*, Los Angeles, CA: Feral House.

Bordo, Susan (1999), *The Male Body: A New Look at Men in Public and Private*, New York: Farrar, Straus and Giroux.

Böse, Martina (2003), "Race and Class in the 'Post-Subcultural' Economy" in *The Post-Subcultures Readers*, edited by David Muggleton and Rupert Weinzierl, London: Berg, pp. 167–180.

Boucher, François (1987), *A History of Costume in the West*, London: Thames and Hudson.

Bourdieu, Pierre ([1972] 1977), *Outline of a Theory of Practice*, Cambridge: Cambridge University Press.

Bourdieu, Pierre (1980), *Questions de Sociologies*, Paris: Les Editions de Minuit.

Bourdieu, Pierre (1984), *Distinction: A Social Critique of the Judgment of Taste*, translated by R. Nice, Cambridge: Harvard University Press.

Bourdieu, Pierre (1990), *In Other Worlds*, Stanford, CA: Stanford University Press.

Bourdieu, Pierre (1992), *An Invitation to Reflexive Sociology*, Chicago, IL: University of Chicago Press.

Bourdieu, Pierre (1993), *The Field of Cultural Production*, translated by Philip Richard Nice, Cambridge: Polity.

Boydell, Christine (1996), "The Training Shoe: 'Pump Up the Power'" in *The Gendered Objects*, edited by Pat Kirkham, Manchester: Manchester University Press.

Brake, Michael (1980), *The Sociology of Youth Culture and Youth Subcultures: Sex and Drugs and Rock 'n' Roll?*, London: Routledge & Kegan Paul.

Brake, Michael (1985), *Comparative Youth Culture: The Sociology of Youth Cultures and Youth Subcultures in America, Britain and Canada*, London: Routledge & Kegan Paul Ltd.

Brenninkmeyer, Ingrid (1963), *The Sociology of Fashion*, Köln-Opladen, Germany: Westdeutscher Verlag.

Breward, Christopher (1999), *The Hidden Consumer: Masculinities, Fashion and City Life 1860–1914*, Manchester: Manchester University Press.

Breward, Christopher (2004), *Fashioning London: Clothing and the Modern Metropolis*, Oxford: Berg.

Breward, Christopher (2011), "Fashioning Masculinity: Men's Footwear and Modernity" in *Shoes: A History from Sandals to Sneakers*, edited by Giorgio Riello and Peter McNeil, Paperback Edition, London: Berg, pp. 206–223.

Brill, Dunja (2007), "Gender, Status and Subcultural Capital in the Goth Scene" in *Youth Cultures: Scenes, Subcultures and Tribes*, edited by Paul Hodkinson and Wolfgang Deicke, London: Routledge, pp. 111–126.

Brooke, Iris (1972), *Footwear: A Short History of European and American Shoes*, London: Pitman Publishing.

Brooker, Peter and Will Brooker (1997), "Introduction" in *Postmodern After-Images*, edited by Peter Brooker and Will Brooker, London: Edward Arnold, pp. 1–19.

Brown, Andy (2007), "Rethinking the Subcultural Commodity: The Case of the Heavy Metal T-shirt Culture(s)" in *Youth Cultures: Scenes, Subcultures and Tribes*, edited by Paul Hodkinson and Wolfgang Deicke, New York: Routledge, pp. 63–78.

Brummel, Beau ([1932] 1972), *Male and Female Costume: Grecian and Roman Costume, British Costume from the Roman Invasion until 1822, and the Principles of Costume Applied to the Improved Dress of the Present Day*, New York: Benjamin Blom, Inc.

Buchanan, Richard (1995), "Rhetoric, Humanism, and Design" in *Discovering Design: Explorations in Design Studies*, edited by Richard Buchanan and Victor Margolin, Chicago, IL: University of Chicago Press, pp. 23–55.

Buchanan, Richard and Victor Margolin (eds.) (1995a), *Exploring Design: Explorations in Design Studies*, Chicago, IL: University of Chicago Press.

Buchanan, Richard and Victor Margolin (1995b), "Introduction" in *Discovering Design: Explorations in Design Studies*, edited by Richard Buchanan, Chicago, IL: University of Chicago Press, pp. ix–xxvi.

Bulmer, Martin (1984), *The Chicago School of Sociology: Institutionalization, Diversity, and the Rise of Sociological Research*, Chicago, IL: University of Chicago Press.

Butler, Judith (1990), *Gender Trouble*, New York: Routledge.

Callahan, Colleen R. and Jo B. Paoletti (2011), "Is It a Girl or a Boy? Gender Identity and Children's Clothing" in *The Fashion Reader*, Second Edition, edited by Linda Welters and Abby Lillethun, Oxford: Berg, pp. 193–196.

Carter, Michael (2003), *Fashion Classics: From Carlyle to Barthes*, London: Berg.

Chaiklin, Martha (2011), "Purity, Pollution and Place in Traditional Japanese Footwear" in *Shoes: A History from Sandals to Sneakers*, edited by Peter McNeil and Giorgio Riello, Paperback Edition, London: Berg, pp. 160–181.

Chang, Jeff (2005), *Can't Stop Won't Stop: A History of the Hip-Hop Generation*, New York: St. Martin's Press.

Chang, Jeff (ed.) (2006a), *Total Chaos: The Art and Aesthetics of Hip-Hop*, New York: BasicCivitas.

Chang, Jeff (2006b), "Codes and the B-Boy's Stigmata: An Interview with DOZE" in *Total Chaos: The Art and Aesthetics of Hip-Hop*, edited by Jeff Chang, New York: Basic Civitas, pp. 321–330.

Chernikowski, Stephanie (1997), *Blank Generation Revisited: The Early Days of Punk Rock*, New York: Schirmer Books.

Choklat, Aki (2012), *Footwear Design*, London: Laurence King Publishing.

Choklat, Aki and Rachel Jones (eds.) (2009), *Shoe Design*, Cologne, Germany: Fusion Publishing.

Clark, Dylan (2003), "The Death and Life of Punk, the Last Subculture" in *The Post-Subcultures Readers*, edited by David Muggleton and Rupert Weinzierl, London: Berg, pp. 223–236.

Clarke, John, Stuart Hall, Tony Jefferson and Brian Roberts (1976), "Subcultures, Cultures and Class" in *Resistance Through Rituals: Youth Subcultures in Post-War Britain*, edited by Stuart Hall and Tony Jefferson, London: Hutchinson, pp. 9–74.

Cloward, Richard and Lloyd Ohlin (1961), *Delinquency and Opportunity: A Theory of Delinquent Gangs*, Glencoe, IL: Free Press.

Cogan, Brian (2006), *Encyclopedia of Punk Music and Culture*, Westport, CT: Greenwood Press.

Cohen, Albert K. (1955). *Delinquent Boys: The Culture of the Gang*, Glencoe, IL: Free Press.

Cohen, Albert (1970), "A General Theory of Subcultures" in *The Sociology of Subcultures*, edited by D. O. Arnold, Berkeley, CA: The Glendessary Press.

Cohen, Phil (1972), *Sub-Cultural Conflict and Working Class Community. Working Papers in Cultural Studies.*No. 2, Birmingham: University of Birmingham.

Colatrella, Carol (2011), *Toys and Tools in Pink: Cultural Narratives of Gender, Science and Technology*, Ohio: Ohio State University Press.

Cole, Robert J. (1989), "Japanese Buy New York Cachet with Deal for Rockefeller Center", *The New York Times*, October 31.

Collins, Jim (1989), *Uncommon Cultures: Popular Culture and Post-Modernism*, New York: Routledge.

Collins, Randall (1981), *Conflict Sociology*, New York: Academic Press.

Connell, R. W. (1987), *Gender and Power*, Stanford, CA: Stanford University Press.

Considine, Austin (2012), "When Sneakers and Race Collide", *The New York Times*, June 20, p. E7.

Craik, Jennifer (1994), *The Face of Fashion*, London: Routledge.

Crane, Diana (1987), *The Transformation of the Avant-Garde: The New York Art World 1940–1985*, Chicago, IL: University of Chicago Press.

Crane, Diana (1992), "High Culture Versus Popular Culture Revisited" in *Cultivating Differences: Symbolic Boundaries and the Making of Inequality*, edited by Michèle Lamont and Marcel Fournier, Chicago, IL: University of Chicago Press, pp. 58–73.

Crane, Diana (1993), "Fashion Design as an Occupation", *Current Research on Occupations and Professions*, 8: 55–73.

Crane, Diana (1994), "Introduction: The Challenge of the Sociology of Culture to Sociology as a Discipline" in *The Sociology of Culture*, edited by Diana Crane, Oxford: Blackwell.

Crane, Diana (1997a), "Globalization, Organizational Size, and Innovation in the French Luxury Fashion Industry: Production of Culture Theory Revisited", *Poetics*, 24: 393–414.

Crane, Diana (1997b), "Postmodernism and the Avant-Garde: Stylistic Change in Fashion Design", *MODERNISM/Modernity*, 4: 123–140.

Crane, Diana (1999), "Diffusion Models and Fashion: A Reassessment in the Social Diffusion of Ideas and Things", *The Annals of the Academy of Political and Social Science*, 566, November: 13–24.

Crane, Diana (2000), *Fashion and Its Social Agendas: Class, Gender, and Identity in Clothing*, Chicago, IL: The University of Chicago Press.

Csikszentmihalyi, Mihaly and Eugene Rochberg-Halton (1981), *The Meaning of Things: Domestic Symbols and the Self*, Cambridge: Cambridge University Press.

Davidson, Hilary (2011), "Sex and Sin: The Magic of Red Shoes" in *Shoes: A History from Sandals to Sneakers*, edited by Peter McNeil and Giorgio Riello, Paperback Edition, London: Berg, pp. 272–289.

Davis, Fred (1985), "Clothing and Fashion as Communication" in *The Psychology of Fashion*, edited by Michael R. Solomon, Lexington: Lexington Books.

Davis, Fred (1992), *Fashion, Culture, and Identity*, Chicago, IL: The University of Chicago Press.

De La Haye, Amy and Cathie Dingwall (1996), *Surfers, Soulies, Skinheads and Skaters: Subcultural Style of the Forties to the Nineties*, Woodstock, NY: Overlook.

DeCerteau, Michel (1984), *The Practice of Everyday Life*, Berkeley, CA: University of California Press.

DeMello, Margo (2009), *Feet and Footwear: A Cultural Encyclopedia*, Westport, CT: Greenwood.

Desideri, Ippolito (2010), *Mission to Tibet: The Extraordinary Eighteenth-Century Account of Father Ippolito Desideri, S.J.*, edited by Leonard Zwilling and translated by Michael J. Sweet, Boston, MA: Wisdom Publications.

DiMaggio, Paul (1992), "Cultural Entreneurship in 19th Century Boston" in *Cultivating Differences: Symbolic Boundaries and the Making of Inequality*, edited by Michèle Lamont and Marcel Fournier, Chicago, IL: The University of Chicago Press.

DiMaggio, Paul and Michael Useem (1978), "Cultural Democracy in a Period of Cultural Expansion: The Social Composition of Arts Audiences in the United States", *Social Problems*, 26: 2.

Docker, John (1994), *Postmodernism and Popular Culture*, Cambridge: Cambridge University Press.

Douglas, Mary (1978), *Cultural Bias*, London: Routledge and Kegan Paul.

Drake, Kate (2001), "Quest for Kawaii", *Time International*, June 25, p. 46.

Duncan, Hugh Dalziel (1969), *Symbols and Social Theory*, New York: Oxford University Press.

Durkheim, Emile ([1893] 1964), *The Division of Labor*, New York: Free Press.

Durkheim, Emile ([1895] 1961), *Rules of the Sociological Method*, New York: Free Press.

Durkheim, Emile ([1897] 1951), *Suicide*, translated by John Spaulding and George Simpson, Glencoe, IL: The Free Press.

Durkheim, Emile ([1912] 1965), *The Elementary Forms of Religious Life*, New York: Collier Books.

Dyson, Michael Eric (1993), *Reflecting Black: African-American Cultural Criticism*, St. Paul, MN: University of Minnesota Press.

Eagleton, Terry (1983), *Literary Theory: An Introduction*, Oxford: Blackwell Publishing.

Edwards, Tim (1997), *Men in the Mirror: Men's Fashion, Masculinity and Consumer Society*, London: Cassell.

Edwards, Tim (2006), *Cultures of Masculinity*, London: Routledge.

Eicher, Joanne B. (1969), *African Dress; A Selected and Annotated Bibliography of Subsaharan Countries*, East Lansing, MI: African Studies Center, Michigan State University.

Eicher, Joanne B. (1976), *Nigerian Handcrafted Textiles*, Ile-Ife, Nigeria: University of Ife Press.

Eicher, Joanne B. (ed.) (1995), *Dress and Ethnicity: Change Across Space and Time*, Oxford: Berg.

Eicher, Joanne B. and Lidia Sciama (1998), *Beads and Bead Makers: Gender, Material Culture, and Meaning*, Oxford: Berg.

Eicher, Joanne B. and Mary Ellen Roach (eds) (1965), *Dress, Adornment, and the Social Order*, New York: Wiley.

Eicher, Joanne B. and Ruth Barnes (1992), *Dress and Gender: Making and Meaning in Cultural Contexts*, Oxford: Berg.

Eicher, Joanne B., Sandra Lee Evenson and Hazel A. Lutz (eds) (2008), *The Visible Self: Global Perspectives on Dress, Culture, and Society*, New York: Fairchild Publications, Inc.

Entwistle, Joanne (2006), "The Cultural Economy of Buying" in Patrik Aspers and Lise Skov, *Current Sociology*, 54, 5: 704–724, Thousand Oaks, CA: Sage.

Entwistle, Joanne (2009), *The Aesthetic Economy of Fashion*, Oxford: Berg.

Ewen, Stuart (1976), *Captains of Consciousness: Advertising and the Social Roots of the Consumer Culture*, New York: McGraw-Hill.

Farrelly, Liz (2005), *Fashion Forever: 30 Years of Subculture*, Philadelphia, PA: Trans-Atlantic Publications.

Featherstone, Mike (2007), *Consumer Culture and Postmodernism*, London: Sage.

Feldman, Christine Jacqueline (2009), *"We are the Mods": A Transnational History of a Youth Subculture*, New York: Peter Lang.

Feldman, Jessica R. (1993), *Gender on the Divide: The Dandy in Modernist Literature*, Ithaca, NY: Cornell University Press.

Fillin-Yeh, Susan (ed.) (2001), *Dandies: Fashion and Finesse in Art and Culture*, New York: New York University Press.

Finkelstein, Joanne (1996), *After a Fashion*, Carlton, Australia: Melbourne University Press.

Fischer, Claude Serge (1972), "Urbanism as a Way of Life- a Review and an Agenda", *Sociological Methods and Research*, 1, 2, November: 187–243.

Fischer, Claude Serge (1975), "Towards a Subcultural Theory of Urbanism", *American Journal of Sociology*, 80, 6: 1319–1341.

Fiske, John (1989), *Reading the Popular*, London: Routledge.

Flügel, J. C. (1930), *The Psychology of Clothes*, London: Hogarth.

Flügel, J. C. (1934), *Men and Their Motives: Psycho-Analytical Studies*, London: Kegan Paul, Trench, Trubner & Co.

Forman, Murray and Mark Anthony Neal (eds) (2004), *That's the Joint!:The Hip-Hop Studies Reader*, New York: Routledge.

Frazer, Edward Franklin (1939), *The Negro Family in the United States*, Chicago, IL: University of Chicago Press.

Friedan, Betty (1963), *The Feminine Mystique*, New York: W.W. Norton.

Gans, Herbert (1975), *Popular Culture and High Culture: An Analysis and Evaluation of Taste*, New York: Basic Books.

Garber, Margaret (1992), *Vested Interests: Cross-Dressing and Cultural Anxiety*, New York: Routledge.

Garcia, Bobbito (2003), *Where'd You Get Those? New York City's Sneaker Culture: 1960–1987*, New York: Testify Books.

Garret, Ruth Irene and Ottie Garret (2003), *My Amish Heritage*, Nashville, TN: Turner Publishing.

Geertz, Clifford ([1973] 1975), *The Interpretation of Culture*, London: Hutchinson.

Gelder, Ken (ed.) (2005a), *The Subcultures Reader*, London: Routledge.

Gelder, Ken (ed.) (2005b), "Introduction: The Field of Subculture Studies" in *The Subcultures Reader*, edited by Ken Gelder, London: Routledge, pp. 1–18.

Gelder, Ken (ed.) (2007), *Subcultures: Cultural Histories and Social Practice*, London: Routledge.

Giddens, Anthony (1991), *Modernity and Self-Identity*, Palo Alto, CA: Stanford University Press.

Gilbert, James (2005), *Men in the Middle: Searching for Masculinity in the 1950s*, Chicago, IL: University of Chicago Press.

Gill, Alison (2011), "Limousines for the Feet: The Rhetoric of Sneakers" in *Shoes: A History from Sandals to Sneakers*, edited by Peter McNeil and Giorgio Riello, Paperback Edition, London: Berg, pp. 372–85.

Gilroy, Paul (1991), *"There Ain't No Black in the Union Jack!": The Cultural Politics of Race and Nation*, Chicago, IL: University of Chicago.

Gilroy, Paul (1993), *The Black Atlantic: Modernity and Double Consciousness*, Cambridge, MA: Harvard University Press.

Gilroy, Paul (2002), *Against Race: Imagining Political Culture Beyond the Color Line*, Cambridge, MA: Harvard University Press.

Glickson, Grant (2014), "At 'Sneakerhead' Fairs, Air Jordans Are Golden", *The New York Times*, April 17, p. A1.

Godart, Frédéric (2012), *Unveiling Fashion: Business, Culture, and Identity, in the Most Glamorous Industry*, New York: Palgrave Macmillan.

Goffman, Erving (1959), *The Presentation of Self in Everyday Life*, Garden City, NY: Doubleday.

Goffman, Erving (1979), *Gender Advertisements*, Cambridge, MA: Harvard University Press, (Hardcover, New York: Harper and Row).

Gordon, Milton M. (1947), "The Concept of Subculture and Its Application", *Social Forces*, 26: 40–42.

Gramsci, Antonio ([1929–1933] 1992), *Prison Notebooks, Volume 1*, New York: Columbia University Press.

Grew, Francis and Margarethe De Neergaard (1988), *Shoes and Patters: Medieval Finds from Excavations in London*, London: Her Majesty's Stationery Office.

Griffin, Chris E. (2011), "The Trouble with Class: Researching Youth, Class and Culture Beyond the 'Birmingham School'", *Journal of Youth Studies*, 14, 3: 245–259.

Habraken, William (Boy) (2000), *Tribal and Ethnic Footwear of the World: Mocassins, Sandals, Clogs, Slippers, Boots and Shoes*, Oosterhout, Holland: LSC Communicatie bv.

Haenfler, Ross (2006), *Straight Edge: Clear-Living Youth, Hardcore Punk and Social Change*, New Brunswick, NJ: Rutgers University Press.

Haenfler, Ross (2009), *Goths, Gamers, and Grrrls: Deviance and Youth Subcultures*, New York: Oxford University Press.

Haenfler, Ross (2014), *Subcultures: The Basics*, New York: Routledge.

Halberstam, Judith (1998), *Female Masculinity*, Durham, NC: Duke University Press.

Hald, Margrethe (1972), *Primitive Shoes: An Archaeological-Ethnological Study Based Upon Shoe Finds from the Jutland Peninsula*, Copenhagen, Denmark: The National Museum of Denmark.

Hall, Stuart (1980a), "Cultural Studies and the Centre: Some Problematics and Problems" in *Culture, Media, Language*, edited by Stuart Hall, Dorothy Hobson, Andrew Lower and Paul Willis, London: Unwin Hyman.

Hall, Stuart (1980b), "Encoding/Decoding" in *Culture, Media, Language*, edited by Stuart Hall, Dorothy Hobson, Andrew Lower and Paul Willis, London: Unwin Hyman.

Hall, Stuart (1992), "The Question of Cultural Identity" in *Modernity and Its Futures*, edited by Stuart Hall and Tony McGrew, Cambridge: Polity Press, pp. 273–323.

Hall, Stuart and Tony Jefferson (eds) (1976), *Resistance Through Rituals: Youth Subcultures in Post-War Britain*, London: Hutchinson.

Harris, Anita (2007), *Next Wave Cultures: Feminism, Subcultures, Activism*, London: Routledge.

Harris, Cheryl and Alison Alexander (1998), *Theorizing Fandom: Fans, Subculture and Identity*, Cresskill, NJ: Hampton Press.

Harris, David (1992), *From Class Struggle to the Politics of Pleasure*, London: Routledge.

Harvey, David (1989), *The Condition of Postmodernity*, Oxford: Blackwell.

Heard, Neal (2003), *The Trainers: Over 300 Classics from Rare Vintage to the Latest Designs*, London: Carlton Book.

Heard, Neal (2009), *Sneakers (Special Limited Edition): Over 300 Classics from Rare Vintage to the Latest Designs*, London: Carlton Books.

Heard, Neal (2012), *The Sneaker Hall of Fame: All-Time Favorite Footwear Brands*, London: Carlton Books.

Hebdige, Dick (1979), *Subculture: The Meaning of Style*, Routledge: London and New York.

Hebdige, Dick (1986), "Postmodernism and the Other Side", *Journal of Communication*, 10, 2: 78–89.

Hebdige, Dick (1988), *Hiding in the Light: On Images and Things*, London: Routledge.

Herc, D. J. Kool (2005), "Introduction" in *Can't Stop Won't Stop: A History of the Hip-Hop Generation*, edited by Jeff Chang, New York: St. Martin's Press, pp. xi–xiii.

Heylin, Clinton (1993), *From the Velvets to the Voidoids: A Pre-Punk History for a Post-Punk World*, New York: Penguin Books.

Hjorth, Larissa (2005), "Odours of Mobility: Mobile Phones and Japanese Cute Culture in the Asia-Pacific", *Journal of Intercultural Studies* 26, February–May: 39–55.

Hodkinson, Paul (2002), *Goth: Identity, Style and Subculture*, Oxford: Berg.

Hoggart, Richard (1957), *The Uses of Literacy*, London: Chatto and Windus.

Hollander, Anne (1994), *Sex and Suits*, New York: A.A. Knopf.

Hulsbosch, Marianne (2014), *Pointy Shoes and Pith Helmets: Dress and Identity Construction in Ambon from 1850–1942*, Leiden, The Netherlands: Brill.

Hume, Lynne (2013), *The Religious Life of Dress: Global Fashion and Faith*, London: Bloomsbury.

Huyssen, Andreas (1986), *After the Great Divide: Modernism, Mass Culture and Postmodernism*, Basingstoke: Macmillan.

Intercity (2008), *Art and Sole: Contemporary Sneaker Art & Design*, London: Laurence King.

Irwin, John ([1970] 2005), "Notes on the Status of the Concept Subculture" in *The Subcultures Reader*, Second Edition, edited by Ken Gelder, London: Routledge, pp. 73–80.

Issitt, Micah L. (2009), *Hippies: A Guide to an American Subculture*, Westport, CT: Greenwood.

Jackson, Beverly (1997), *Splendid Slippers: A Thousand Years of an Erotic Tradition*, Berkeley, CA: Ten Speed Press.

Jackson, Scoop (2013), "Nike. Bball. Dominance" in *SLAM KICKS*, edited by Ben Osborne, New York: Universe Publishing.

Jain-Neubauer, Jutta (2000), *Feet & Footwear in Indian Culture*, Toronto, Canada: The Bata Shoe Museum with Mapin Publishing Pvt. Ltd, Ahmedabad.

Jameson, Fredric (1983), "Postmodernism and Consumer Society" in *The Anti-Aesthetic: Essays on Postmodern Culture*, edited by H. Foster, Seattle, WA: Bay Press.

Jameson, Fredric (1984), "Postmodernism, or the Cultural Logic of Late Capitalism", *New Left Review*, 46: 53–92.

Jeffreys, Sheila (2000), "'Body Art' and Social Status: Cutting, Tattooing and Piercing from a Feminist Perspective", *Feminism & Psychology*, 10, 4: 409–429.

Jenks, Chris (2004), *Subculture: The Fragmentation of the Social*, London: Sage.

Jobling, Paul (2005), *Man Appeal: Advertising, Modernism and Menswear*, Oxford: Berg.

Johnson, Richard (1996), "What Is Cultural Sutides Anyway?" in *What Is Cultural Studies? A Reader*, edited by John Storey, London: Edward Arnold, pp. 75–114.

Jones, Mason, Patrick Macias, Yuji Oniki, and Carl Gustav Horn (1999), *Japan Edge: The Insider's Guide to Japanese Pop Subculture*, San Francisco, CA: Cadence Books.

Jones, Russell M. (2007), *Inside the Graffiti Subculture*, Saarbrücken, Germany: VDM Verlag

Kahn-Harris, Keith (2007), *Extreme Metal: Music and Culture on the Edge*, Oxford: Berg.

Kaplan, Jeffrey (2003), *The Cultic Milieu: Oppositional Subcultures in an Age of Globalization*, Lanham, MD: Rowman Altamira.

Karaminas, Vicki (2009), "Part IV: Subculture: Introduction" in *The Men's Fashion Readers*, edited by Peter McNeil and Vicki Karaminas, Oxford: Berg, pp. 347–351.

Kawamura, Yuniya (2005), *Fashion-ology: An Introduction to Fashion Studies*, Oxford: Berg.

Kawamura, Yuniya (2006a), "Japanese Teens as Producers of Street Fashion" in Patrik Aspers and Lise Skov, *Current Sociology*, 54, 5: 784–801, Thousand Oaks, CA: Sage.

Kawamura, Yuniya (2006b), "Japanese Street Fashion: The Urge to Be Seen and to Be Heard" in *The Fashion Reader*, edited by Linda Welters and Abbey Lillethun, Oxford: Berg.

Kawamura, Yuniya (2010), "Japanese Fashion Subcultures" in *Japan Fashion Now Exhibition Catalogue*, edited by Valerie Steele, New Haven, CT: Yale University Press.

Kawamura, Yuniya (2011), *Doing Research in Fashion and Dress: An Introduction to Qualitative Methods*, Oxford: Berg.

Kawamura, Yuniya (2012), *Fashioning Japanese Subcultures*, London: Berg.

Kelly, Ian (2006), *The Ultimate Man of Style*, New York: Atria Books.

Kidwell, Claudia B. and Valerie Steele (eds) (1989), *Men and Women: Dressing the Part*, Washington, DC: Smithsonian Institution Press.

Kimmel, Michael (2012), *The Gendered Society*, New York: Oxford University Press.

Kirkham, Pat (ed.) (1996), *The Gendered Object*, Manchester: Manchester University Press.

Ko, Dorothy (2001), *Every Step a Lotus: Shoes for Bound Feet*, Berkeley, CA: University of California Press.

Koda, Harold (2001), *Extreme Beauty: The Body Transformed. Exhibition Catalogue*. New Haven, CT: Yale University Press.

Koenig, Rene (1973), *A La Mode: On the Social Psychology of Fashion*, New York: Seabury Press.

Kuchta, Davis (2002), *The Three-Piece Suit and Modern Masculinity: England, 1550–1850*, Berkeley, CA: University of California Press.

Kunzle, David (2004), *Fashion & Fetishism*, London: Sutton Publishing.

Lamy, Philip and Jack Levin (1985), "Punk and Middle-Class Values: A Content Analysis", *Youth Society*, 17: 157–170.

Lang, Kurt and Gladys Engel Lang (1961), *Collective Dynamics*, New York: Thomas Y. Crowell, pp. 486–471.

Lash, Scott (1990), *Sociology of Postmodernism*, London: Routledge.

Laver, James (1968), *Dandies*, London: Weidenfeld & Nicolson.

Laver, James (1979), *The Concise History of Costume and Fashion*, New York: Abrams.

Lawlor, Laurie (1996), *Where Will This Shoe Take You?: A Walk through the History of Footwear*, New York: Walker and Company.

Lazenby, Roland (2014), *Michael Jordan: The Life*, New York: Little, Brown and Company.

Leblanc, Lauraine (1999), *Pretty in Punk: Girls' Gender Resistance in a Boys' Subculture*, New Brunswick, NJ: Rutgers University Press.

Ledger, Florence (1978), *Put Your Foot Down: A Treatise on the History of Shoes*, New York: Colin Venton.

Legates, Marlene (2001), *In Their Time: A History of Feminism in Western Society*. New York: Longman Publishing Group.

Lemert, Charles (1997), *Postmodernism Is Not What You Think*, Oxford: Blackwell.

Lerman, Nina and Ruth Oldenziel (eds) (2003), *Gender and Technology: A Reader*, John Hopkins University Press.

Liebow, Elliot (1967), *Tally's Corner: A Study of Negro Street Corner*, Boston, MA: Little, Brown and Company.

Lillethun, Abby (2011), "Part IV-Fashion and Identity: Introduction" in *The Fashion Reader*, Second Edition, edited by Linda Welters and Abby Lillethun, Oxford: Berg, pp. 189–191.

Lipovetsky, Gilles (1994), *Empire of Fashion: Dressing Modern Democracy*, Princeton, NJ: Princeton University Press.

Longeville, Thibaut de and Lisa Leone (dir.) (2005), *Just for Kicks*, DVD.

Lovell, Terry (1998), "Cultural Production" in *Cultural Theory and Popular Culture: A Reader*, edited by John Storey, Hemel Hempstead: Prentice Hall, pp. 476–482.

Lukács, Georg (1971), *History and Class Consciousness*, London: Merlin Press.

Luvaas, Brent (2012), *DIY Style: Fashion, Music and Global Digital Cultures*, London: Berg.

Lv, Luo and Zhang Huiguang (2007), *Sneakers*, Victoria, BC: Page One Publishing.

Lyotard, Jean-François (1984), *The Postmodern Condition*, translated by Geoffrey Bennington and Brian Massumi, Manchester: Manchester University Press.

MacDonald, Dwight (1998), "A Theory of Mass Culture" in *Cultural Theory and Popular Culture: A Reader*, edited by John Storey, Hemel Hempstead: Prentice Hall, pp. 22–36.

MacDonald, Nancy (2003), *The Graffiti Subculture: Youth, Masculinity and Identity in London and New York*, New York: Palgrave.

MacRae, Rhoda (2007), "'Insider' and 'Outsider' Issues in Youth Research" in *Youth Cultures: Scenes, Subcultures and Tribes*, edited by Paul Hodkinson and Wolfgang Deicke, London: Routledge, pp. 51–61.

Martin-Barbero, Jesus (1993), *Communication, Culture and Hegemony*, London: Sage.

Martinez, Katharine and Kenneth L. Ames (1997), *The Material Culture of Gender, the Gender of Material Culture*, Winterhur, DEL: The Henry Francis du Pont Winterhur Museum.

Marx, Karl (1956), *Capital*, Moscow: Progress Publishers.

Mattioli, Dana (2011), "Nike Footwork Yields Long Lines", *The Wall Street Journal*, December 29.

McCracken, Grant (1988), *Culture and Consumption: New Approaches to the Symbolic Character of Consumer Goods and Activities*, Bloomington, IN and Indianapolis, IN: Indiana University Press.

McDowell, Colin (1989), *Shoes: Fashion and Fantasy*, London: Thames and Hudson Ltd.

McIver, Jack Alexander (1994), *All About Shoes: Footwear Through the Ages*, Toronto, Canada: Bata Limited.

McLung, Alfred Lee (1945), *Race Riots Aren't Necessary*, New York: Public Affairs Committee, Inc.

McNeil, Peter (2009), "Part I: A Brief History of Men's Fashion - Introduction" in *The Men's Fashion Readers*, edited by Peter McNeil and Vicki Karaminas, Oxford: Berg, pp. 15–18.

McNeil, Peter and Giorgio Riello (eds) (2011a), *Shoes: A History from Sandals to Sneakers*, Paperback Edition, London: Berg

McNeil, Peter and Giorgio Riello (eds) (2011b), "A Long Walk: Shoes, People and Place" in *Shoes: A History from Sandals to Sneakers*, Paperback Edition, London: Berg, pp. 2–28.

McNeil, Peter and Giorgio Riello (eds) 2011c), "Walking the Streets of London and Paris: Shoes in the Enlightenment" in *Shoes: A History from Sandals to Sneakers*, Paperback Edition, London: Berg, pp. 94–115.

McNeil, Peter and Vicki Karaminas (eds) (2009), *The Men's Fashion Reader*, London: Berg.

McRobbie, Angela (1981), "Settling Accounts with Subcultures: A Feminist Critique" in *Culture, Ideology, and Social Process*, edited by Tony Bennet, Graham Martin, Colin Mercer and Janet Woollacott, London: Open University Press.

McRobbie, Angela ([1989] 2005), "Second-Hand Dresses and the Role of the Ragmarket" in *The Subcultures Reader*, edited by Ken Gelder, New York: Routledge.

McRobbie, Angela (1991), *Feminism and Youth Culture: From "Jackie" to "Just Seventeen"*, London: Macmillan

McRobbie, Angela and Jennifer Gerber ([1981] 1991), "Girls and Subcultures" in *Feminism and Youth Culture: From "Jackie" to "Just Seventeen"*, edited by Angela McRobbie, London: Macmillan.

McRobbie, Angela and Mica Nava (eds.) (1984), *Gender and Generation*, London: Macmillan.

McWilliams, John C. (2000), *The 1960s Cultural Revolution*, Westport, CT: Greenwood.

Mead, Margaret (1935), *Sex and Temperament in Three Primitive Societies*, New York: George Routledge.

Merton, Robert K. (1946), *Mass Persuasion*, New York: Harper and Bros.

Merton, Robert K. (1957), *Social Theory and Social Structure*, New York: Free Press.

Messner, Michael (2000), "Barbie Girls Versus Sea Monsters", *Gender and Society Journal*, 14, 6: 765–784.

Miller, Judith (2009), *Shoes*, New York: Octopus Publishing.

Miller, Monica L. (2013), "'Fresh-Dressed Like a Million Bucks': Black Dandyism and Hip-Hop" in *Artist, Rebel, Dandy: Men of Fashion*, edited by Kate Irvin and Laurie Anne Brewer, New Haven, CT: Yale University Press, in association with Museum of Art, Rhode Island School of Design, pp. 149–158.

Mills, C. Wright (1959), *The Sociological Imagination*, Oxford: Oxford University Press.

Mills, Ron and Allen Huff (1999), *Style Over Substance: A Critical Analysis of an African-American Teenage Subculture*, Chicago, IL: African American Images.

Mitchell, Louise (ed.) (2006), *The Cutting Edge: Fashion from Japan*, Sydney, Australia: Museum of Applied Arts and Sciences.

Moore, Ryan (2009), *Sells Like Teen Spirit: Youth Culture and Social Crisis*, New York: NYU Press.

Morales, Marta (2013), *The Complete Book of Shoes*, New York: Firefly Books Ltd.

Muggleton, David (1997), "The Post-Subculturalist" in *The Clubcultures Reader: Readings in Popular Cultural Studies*, edited by Steve Redhead, Derek Wynne, and Justin O'Connor, Oxford: Blackwell.

Muggleton, David (2000), *Inside Subculture: The Postmodern Meaning of Style*, Oxford: Berg.

Muggleton, David and Rupert Weinzierl (eds.) (2003), *The Post-Subcultures Reader*, Oxford: Berg.

Muller, Florence (1997), *Baskets: Une historie des chaussures de sport, de ville*, Paris: Editions du Regard.

Nahshon, Edna (2008), "Jews and Shoes" in *Jews and Shoes*, edited by Edna Nahshon, Oxford: Berg, pp. 1–36.

Nava, Mica (1992), *Changing Cultures: Feminism, Youth Consumerism*, London: Sage.

Ogunnaike, Lola (2004), "SoHo Runs for Blue and Yellow Sneakers", *The New York Times*, December 19.

O'Hara, Craig (2001), *The Philosophy of Punk: More Than Noise*, San Francisco, CA: AK Press.

O'Keefe, Linda (1996), *Shoes: A Celebration of Pumps, Sandals, Slippers and More*, New York: Workman Publishing Company.

Osborne, Ben (ed.) (2014), *SLAM KICKS: Basketball Sneakers that Changed the Game*, New York: Universe Publishing.

Osgerby, Bill (1998), *Youth in Britain Since 1945*, Oxford: Blackwell Publishing Ltd.

Ouaknin, Marc-Alain (2000), *Symbols of Judaism*, Paris, France: Assouline Publishing.

Palazzolo, Joe (2014), "Do Jurors Have a Right to Wear Sneakers?", *The Wall Street Journal* blog, June 9 (blogs.wsj.com/law/author/jpalazzolo).

Palladini, Doug (2009), *Vans "Off the Wall": Stories of Sole from Vans Originals*, New York: Abrams.

Paris, Jeffrey and Michael Ault (2004), "Subcultures and Political Resistance", *Peace Review*, 16, 4: 403–407.

Parmar, Priya, Birgit Richard and Shirley R. Steinberg (2006), *Contemporary Youth Culture: An International Encyclopedia*, Westport, CT: Greenwood.

Patton, Paul (1986), "The Selling of Michael Jordan", *New York Times Magazine*, November 9: 48–58.

Payne, Blanche (1965), *History of Costume from the Ancient Egyptians to the Twentieth Century*, New York: Harper & Row.

Peck & Snyder (1971), *Sporting Goods*, Princeton, NJ: The Pyne Press.

Peng, Hsiao-yen (2010), *Dandyism and Transcultural Modernity: The Dandy, the Flaneur, and the Translator in 1930s Shanghai, Tokyo and Paris*, London: Routledge.

Perrot, Philip (1996), *Fashioning the Bourgeoisie: A History of Clothing in the Nineteenth Century*, translated by Richard Bienvenu, Princeton, NJ: Princeton University Press.

Peterson, Hal (2007), *Chucks! The Phenomenon of Converse Chuck Taylor All Star*, New York: Skyhorse Publishing.

Peterson, Richard A. (1992), "Understanding Audience Segmentation: From Elite and Mass to Omnivore and Univore", *Poetics*, 21: 243–258.

Peterson, Richard A. and Roger M. Kern (1996), "Changing Highbrow Taste: From Snob to Omnivore", *American Sociological Review*, 61: 900–907.

Pilkington, Hilary (1994), *Russia's Youth and Its Culture: A Nation's Constructor and Constructed*, London: Routledge.

Pilkington, Hilary (1996), *Gender, Generation and Identity in Contemporary Russia*, London: Routledge.

Pilkington, Hilary and Galina Yemelianova (eds) (2002), *Islam in Post-Soviet Russia*, London: Routledge.

Pilkington, Hilary Al'bina Garifzianova and Elena Omel'chenko (2010), *Russia's Skinheads: Exploring and Rethinking Subcultural Lives*, London: Routledge.

Ping, Wang (2002), *Aching for Beauty: Footbinding in China*, New York: Anchor Books.

Polhemus, Ted (1994), *Street Style*, London: Thames and Hudson.

Polhemus, Ted (1996), *Style Surfing*, London: Thames and Hudson.

Polhemus, Ted and Lynn Proctor (1978), *Fashion and Antifashion: An Anthropology of Clothing and Adornment*, London: Thames and Hudson.

Prasso, Sheridan and Diane Brady (2003), "Can the High End Hold Its Own?", *Business Week*, June 30, p. 7.

Price, Emmett G. III (2006), *Hip-Hop Culture*, Santa, CA: ABC-CLIO, Inc.

Purcell, Natalie J. (2003), *Death Metal Music: The Passion and Politics of a Subculture*, Jefferson, NC: McFarland.

Rabaka, Reiland (2011), *Hip Hop's Inheritance: From the Harlem Renaissance to the Hip Hop Feminist Movement*, Lanham, MD: Rowman and Littlefield Publishers.

Raha, Maria (2005), *Cinderella's Big Score: Women of the Punk and Indie Underground*, Emeryville, CA: Sea Press.

Rahn, Janice (2002), *Painting Without Permission: Hip-Hop Graffiti Subculture*, Westport, CT: Bergin & Garvey

Readhead, Steve (1997), *Subculture to Clubcultures: An Introduction to Popular Cultural Studies*, Oxford: Blackwell Publishing.

Reddington, Helen (2004), "The Forgotten Revolution of Female Punk Musicians in the 1970s", *Peace Review*, 16, 4: 439–444.

Reed, John Shelton (1972), *The Enduring South: Subcultural Persistence in Mass Society*. Lexington, MA: D.C. Health.

Reilly, Andrew and Sarah Cosbey (2008), *Men's Fashion Reader*, New York: Fairchild Books.

Riello, Giorgio (2006), *A Foot in the Past*, London: Oxford University Press.

Roach-Higgins, Mary Ellen, Joanne B. Eicher and Kim K. P. Johnson (1995), *Dress and Identity*, New York: Fairchild.

Robertson, Roland (1995), "Glocalization: Time-Space and Homogeneity-Heterogeneity" in *Global Modernities*, edited by Mike Featherstone, Scott Lash and Robert Robertson, London: Sage, pp. 25–44.

Robinson, Rebecca (2008), "It Won't Stop: The Evolution of Men's Hip-Hop Gear" in *Men's Fashion Reader*, edited by Andrew Reilly and Sarah Cosbey, New York: Fairchild Books, pp. 253–263.

Rocca, Federico (2013), *A Matter of Fashion: 20 Iconic Items that Changed the History of Style*, New York: White Star Publishers.

Roche, Daniel (1997), *The Culture of Clothing: Dress and Fashion in the Ancient Regime*, translated by Jean Birrell, Cambridge: Cambridge University Press.

Ross, Doran (2011), "Footwear" in *Part 3: Types of Dress in Africa, Volume 1, Berg Encyclopedia of World Dress and Fashion*, edited by Joanne B. Eicher, London: Berg.

Rossi, William A. (1976), *The Sex Life of the Foot and Shoe*, New York: Saturday Review Press.

Sabin, Roger (1999), *Punk Rock: So What?*, New York: Routledge.

Sagert, Kelly Boyer (2009), *Flappers: A Guide to an American Subculture*, Westport, CT: Greenwood.

Said, Edward (1993), *Culture and Imperialism*, New York: Vintage Books.

Sato, Ikuo (1998), *Kamikaze Biker: Parody and Anatomy in Affluent Japan*, Chicago, IL: University of Chicago Press.

Saussure, Ferdinand de ([1916] 1986), *Course in General Linguistics*, La Salle, IL: Open Court Publishing Company.

Schneider, Doug (2008), "Skate Shoes" in *Made for Skate: The Illustrated History of Skateboard Footwear*, edited by Jürgen Blümlein, Daniel Schmid and Dirk Vogel, Berlin, Germany: Gingko Press, p. 59.

Schwöbel, Laura (2008), *Gothic Subculture in Finland: History, Fashion and Lifestyle*, Saarbruecken, Germany: VDM Verlag.

Scott, James. *Domination and the Arts of Resistance*. New Haven, CT: Yale University Press, 1990.

Seidman, Steven (1994), *The Postmodern Turn*, Cambridge: Cambridge University Press.

Semmelhack, Elizabeth (2011), "A Delicate Balance: Women, Power and High Heels" in *Shoes: A History from Sandals to Sneakers*, edited by Peter McNeil and Girogio Riello, Paperback Edition, London: Berg, pp. 224–249.

Shils, Edward (1975a), *Centre and Periphery: Essays in Macrosociology*, Chicago, IL: University of Chicago Press.

Shils, Edward (1975b), *Centre and Periphery: Essays in Macrosociology*, Chicago, IL: University of Chicago Press, pp. 3–16.

Shils, Edward (1975c), *Centre and Periphery: Essays in Macrosociology*, Chicago, IL: University of Chicago Press, pp. 127–134.

Simmel, Georg ([1904] 1957), "Fashion", *The American Journal of Sociology*, LXII, 6, May 1957: 541–558.

Simmel, Georg ([1905] 1997), "Philosophy of Fashion" in *Simmel on Culture*, edited by David Frisby and Michael Featherstone, London: Sage.

Simonelli, David (2002), "Anarchy, Pop and Violence: Punk Rock Subculture and the Rhetoric of Class, 1976-1978", *Contemporary British History*, 16, 2: 121–144.

Sims, Josh (2010), *Cult Street Wear*, London: Laurence King Publishing, Ltd.

Skott-Myhre, Hans Arthur (2009), *Youth and Subculture as Creative Force: Creating New Spaces for Radical Youth Work*, Toronto: University of Toronto Press.

Small, Lisa (ed.) (2014), *Killer Heels: The Art of the High-Heeled Shoe Exhibition Catalogue*, New York: Brooklyn Museum and DelMonico Books.

Smith, Sam (1992), *The Jordan Rules*. New York: Simon and Schuster.

Smith, Sam (2014), *There Is No Next: NBA Legends on the Legacy of Michael Jordan*, New York: Pocket Books Publishing.

Snyder, Gregory J. (2009), *Graffiti Lives: Beyond the Tag in New York's Urban Underground*, New York: New York University Press.

Spencer, Herbert ([1896] 1966), *The Principles of Sociology*, Volume II, New York: D. Appleton and Co.

Stanton, Domna D. (1980), *The Aristocrat as Art: A Study of Honnête Homme and the Dandy in Seventeenth- and Nineteenth-Century French Literature*, New York: Columbia University Press.

Steele, Valerie (1985), *Fashion and Eroticism*, New York: Oxford University Press.

Steele, Valerie (1996), *Fetish: Fashion, Sex, and Power*, Oxford: Oxford University Press.

Steele, Valerie (1999), *Shoes: A Lexicon of Style*, New York: Rizzoli.

Steele, Valerie (2001), *The Corset: A Cultural History*, New Haven, CT and London: Yale University Press.

Steele, Valerie (2011), "Shoes and the Erotic Imagination" in *Shoes: A History from Sandals to Sneakers*, edited by Peter McNeil and Girogio Riello, Paperback Edition, London: Berg, pp. 250–271.

Steele, Valerie (2013), "Introduction" in *Shoe Obsession*, edited by Valerie Steele and Colleen Hill, New Haven, CT: Yale University Press.

Steele, Valerie and Colleen Hill (eds) (2013), *Shoe Obsession*, New Haven, CT: Yale University Press.

Storey, John (1999), *Cultural Consumption and Everyday Life*, London: Arnold.

Storey, John (2001), *Cultural Theory and Popular Culture*, Harlow: Pearson Education.

Storey, John (2003), *Inventing Popular Culture*, Oxford: Blackwell Publishing.

Stroller, Robert (1985), *Observing the Erotic Imagination*, New Haven, CT and London: Yale University Press.

Sumner, William Graham ([1906] 1940), *Folkways: A Study of the Sociological Importance of Usages, Manners, Customs, Mores and Morals*, Boston, MA: Ginn and Company.

Sumner, William Graham and Albert Gallway Keller (1927), *The Science of Society*, Volume III, New Haven, CT: Yale University Press.

Swann, June (1982), *Shoes*, London: Butler & Tanner Ltd.

Swann, June (1986), *Shoemaking*, Princes Risborough: Shire Publications.

Swann, June (2001), *History of Footwear in Norway, Sweden and Finland*, Stockholm, Sweden: Kungl Vitthets Historic och Antikviters.

Tarde, Gabriel (1903), *The Laws of Imitation*, translated by Elsie C. Parsons, New York: Henry Holt.

Thomas, W. I. and Florian Witold Znaniecki (1918), *The Polish Peasant in Europe and America*, Chicago, IL: University of Illinois Press.

Thornton, Sarah (1995), *Club Cultures: Music, Media and Subcultural Capital*, Cambridge: Polity Press.

Thrasher, Frederick M. (1927), *The Gang*, Chicago, IL: University of Chicago Press.

Thuresson, Mike (2002), *"French Fancies", Japan, Inc.*, Tokyo, Japan: SRD Japan Inc.

Tönnies, Ferdinand ([1887] 1963), *Community and Society*, New York: Harper and Row.

Tönnies, Ferdinand ([1909] 1961), *Custom: An Essay on Social Codes*, translated by A. F. Borenstein, New York: The Free Press.

Trasko, Mary (1989), *Heavenly Soles: Extraordinary Twentieth-Century Shoes*, New York: Abbeville Press.

Turcotte, Bryan Ray (2007), *Punk Is Dead, Punk Is Everything*, Corte Madera, CA: Gingko Press.

Turner, Bryan (ed.) (1990), *Theories of Modernity and Postmodernity*, London: Sage.

Turner, Thomas (2013), *The Sports Shoe: A Social and Cultural History, c.1870–c.1990* (unpublished PhD dissertation), Birkbeck, University of London.

Turner, Victor (1986), *The Anthropology of Performance*, New York: PAJ Publications.

U-Dox (2014), *Sneakers: The Complete Limited Editions Guide*, New York: Thames & Hudson.

Unorthdox Styles (2005), *Sneakers: The Complete Collectors' Guide*, New York: Thames and Hudson.

Vainshtein, Olga (2009), "Dandyism, Visual Games, and the Strategies of Representation" in *The Men's Fashion Readers*, edited by Peter McNeil and Vicki Karaminas, Oxford: Berg, pp. 84–107.

Vanderbilt, Tom (1998), *The Sneaker Book: Anatomy of an Industry and an Icon*, New York: The New Press.

Vartanin, Ivan (ed.) (2011a), *High Heels: Fashion, Femininity, Seduction*, Tokyo, Japan: Goliga.

Vartanin, Ivan (2011b), "Introduction: Nude In Heels, or a Fetish for Photography" in *High Heels: Fashion, Femininity, Seduction*, Tokyo, Japan: Goliga, pp. 12–35.

Veblen, Thorstein ([1899] 1957), *The Theory of Leisure Class*, London: Allen and Unwin.

Veblen, Thorstein (1964), "The Economic Theory of Women's Dress" in *Essays in Our Changing Order*, edited by Leon Ardzrooni, New York: Augustus M. Kelley, p. 72.

Vianello, Andrea (2011), "Court Lady or Courtesans? The Venetian Chopine in the Renaissance" in *Shoes: A History from Sandals to Sneakers*, edited by Peter McNeil and Girogio Riello, Paperback Edition, London: Berg, pp. 76–93.

Vogel, Steven (2007), *STREET WEAR: The Insider's Guide*, San Francisco, CA: Chronicle Books.

Walford, Jonathan (2007), *The Seductive Shoe: Four Centuries of Fashion Footwear*, New York: Stewart, Tabori & Chang.

Walford, Jonathan (2010), *Shoes A-Z: Designers, Brands, Manufactures and Retailers*, New York: Thames and Hudson.

Walker, Samuel Americus (1978), *Sneakers*, New York: Workman Publishing.

Walters, Malcolm (1995), *Globalization*, London: Routledge.

Weber, Caroline (2014), "The Eternal High Heel: Eroticism and Empowerment" in *The Killer Heels: The Art of the High-Heeled Shoe Exhibition Catalogue*, edited by Lisa Small, New York: Brooklyn Museum and DelMonico Books.

Weber, Max (1947), *The Theory of Social and Economic Organization*, New York: Oxford University Press.

Weber, Max (1968), *Economy and Society*, New York: Bedminster Press.

Welters, Linda and Abby Lillethun (2011), *The Fashion Reader*, Second Edition, Oxford: Berg

White, Harrison (1993), *Careers and Creativity: Social Forces in the Arts*, Boulder, CO: Westview Press.

White, R. D. (1993), *Youth Subcultures: Theory, History, and the Australian Experience*, Hobart, Tasmania: National Clearinghouse for Youth Studies.

Whyte, William Foote (1943), *Street Corner Society*, Chicago, IL: University of Chicago Press.

Widdicombe, Sue and Rob Wooffitt (1990), "'Being' versus 'Doing' Punk: On Achieving Authenticity as a Member", *Journal of Language and Social Psychology*, 9: 257–277.

Wilcox, Turner (1948), *Mode in Footwear*, New York and London: Charles Scribner's Sons.

Williams, Alex (2012), "Guerilla Fashion: The Story of Supreme", *The New York Times*, November 21, p. E1.

Williams, J. Patrick (2011), *Subcultural Theory: Traditions and Concepts*, Cambridge: Polity Press.

Williams, Raymond (1998), "The Analysis of Culture" in *Cultural Theory and Popular Culture: A Reader*, edited by John Storey, pp. 48–56, Hemel Hempstead: Prentice Hall.

Willis, Paul (1978), *Learning to Labour: How Working Class Kids Get Working Class Jobs*, London: Ashgate Publishing.

Wilson, Elizabeth (1985), *Adorned in Dreams: Fashion and Modernity*, Berkeley, CA: University of California Press.

Wilson, Elizabeth (1994), "Fashion and Postmodernism" in *Cultural Theory and Popular Culture: A Reader*, edited by John Storey, Hemel Hempstead: Prentice Hall, pp. 392–462.

Wilson, Eunice (1969), *A History of Shoe Fashions: A Study of Shoe Design in Relation to Costume for Shoe Designers*, London: Pitman.

Wilson, William Julius (1978), *The Declining Significance of Race*, Chicago, IL: University of Chicago Press.

Wojcik, Daniel (1995), *Punk and Neo-Tribal Body Art*, Jackson, Mississippi: University Press of Mississippi.

Wolfgang, Marvin and Franco Ferracuti (1967), *The Subculture of Violence: Towards an Integrated Theory in Criminology*. London: Tavistock Publications.

Wood, Robert T. (2006), *Straightedge Youth: Complexity and Contradictions of a Subculture*, Syracuse, NY: Syracuse University Press.

Wright, Lee (1989), "Objectifying Gender: The Stiletto Heel" in *A View from the Interior: Feminism, Women and Design*, edited by Judy Atfield and Pat Kirkland, London: The Women's Press, p. 8.

Zamperini, Paola (2011), "A Dream of Butterflies?: Shoes in Chinese Culture" in *Shoes: A History from Sandals to Sneakers*, edited by Peter McNeil and Girogio Riello, Paperback Edition, London: Berg, pp. 196–205.

Zimmerman, Caroline (1978), *The Super Sneaker Book*, New York: A Dolphin Book/ Doubleday & Company, Inc.

INDEX